# Orienteering
for Sport and Pleasure

# Orienteering

## for Sport and Pleasure

### Hans Bengtsson
### & George Atkinson

The Stephen Greene Press   Brattleboro, Vermont

Orienteering *is the trade or service mark of Silva Division of John-
son Diversified, Inc. The authors and publisher are most apprecia-
tive to the people of Silva for their cooperation in its use in connec-
tion with* Orienteering for Sport and Pleasure.

Copyright © 1977 by Hans Bengtsson and George Atkinson

This book has been produced in the United States of America: des gned by
R. L. Dothard Associates, composed by American Book–Stratford Press,
printed and bound by Murray Printing Company. It is published by The
Stephen Greene Press, Brattleboro, Vermont 05301

LIBRARY OF CONGRESS CATALOGING IN PUBLICATION DATA
Bengtsson, Hans, 1937–
    Orienteering for sport and pleasure.
    (Environmental sports series)
    1. Orientation.    I. Atkinson, George, 1947–
joint author.    II. Title.
GV200.4.B46        796.4'2        75-41872
ISBN 0-8289-0271-2
ISBN 0-8289-0270-4 pbk.

77   78   79   80   7   6   5   4   3   2   1

# Contents

# Acknowledgments

The authors wish to express their appreciation to Björn Kjellström, Dr. Howard "Skip" Knuttgen, and the late Sass Peepre, for their contributions to this book and to orienteering.

Further, the publisher and authors wish to make grateful acknowledgment to the many photographers and organizations who have either taken or graciously loaned us the use of their pictures for *Orienteering for Sport and Pleasure*. Special mention should go to the following:

The Swedish Orienteering Federation for their help in supplying the pictures on pages 13, 15, 16 (at right), 21, 29, 41, 69, 105, 129, 186 and 201;

Allan Seymour for the fine photographs he took specifically for this book on pages 18, 28 (at right), 31, 34, 51, 62, 65, 67, 72, 86, 93, 97, 99, 100, 103, 109, 150, 159, 171, 183, 189, 192, 194 and 198;

Jean Davis for her photographs on pages 26, 48, 74 and opposite the title page;

Anders Gade for photographs on pages 8, 11 and 143;

Bob Phillips of Eastman Kodak for the portrait of Björn Kjellström on page 16 at left;

Russell Garland for photos on pages 24, 28 (at left), 98 and 188;

Keith Samuelson for photos on pages 15, 29 and 201;

John Caldwell, Th. Madin, *Skogs Sport* magazine, *Wisconsin Sportsman* magazine, Recreational Equipment, Inc., Pressfoto Meyerhoffer, Aftonbladet and Photo Dalmas for photographs on pages 131, 18, 13, 67, 69, 16, 186 and 105 respectively.

*vi*

The remaining photos are the work of the authors. The diagrams on pages 60 and 74 are drawn by Norman Rogers based on the preparatory work of Hans Bengtsson; the remaining diagrams and spot map drawings are by Hans Bengtsson. The diarama used as background for the photos on pages 51, 86, 97, 99 and 100 was prepared by J. William Hasskarl.

For Lena and Meredith

# Key Word Glossary

*Aiming Off*—plotting a bearing wide of the precise target in a chosen direction to avoid false turns near the mark.

*Attack Point*—a feature from which an orienteer begins to navigate carefully to a *control*.

*Bearing*—a direction of travel usually measured in degrees from North and determined by a map and compass.

*Collecting Feature*—a distinct feature which is relatively easy to find and recognize.

*Control*—a prism-shaped, red and white (almost always) marker placed in the field prior to an orienteering event and corresponding to a known map point; to be located during the event.

*Control Extension*—plotting a course to a larger adjacent feature rather than to the easy-to-miss smaller actual target.

*Handrail*—a feature running parallel to one's direction of travel and thereby serving as a handy navigational aid.

*Knoll*—a small hill.

*Meridian*—lines (real and imaginary respectively) running true North to true South on a map, or the terrain.

*Re-entrant*—in orienteering, an elongated, sloping valley.

*Saddle*—a low point on a ridge connecting two summits.

*Spur*—a narrow, sloping ridge.

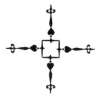

# O for Orienteering

**Y**OU ARE MOVING quickly and quietly through the beautiful forest valley. After jumping the small stream, you focus your attention on the wooded hillside above you. Quick measurements are made with your compass. Looking once again to the hillside, you calculate your plan of attack and head for a small rocky outcropping. As you near the rocks, you spot a small, kite-like, red and white nylon marker. That's it! Elation! You're *orienteering*.

Or, after a lazy, successful afternoon of fishing the shores of a remote mountain stream, you reach into your small backpack and pull out a compass and map. Carefully locating your position with the compass, you easily plot your route back to your car, secure also in the knowledge that you'll be able to return to this little-known fishing haven again another day. Congratulations! You're also orienteering.

## Why a book on orienteering?

You may well be asking this question. The answer is easy and becoming more apparent every day.

Orienteering is good, healthy outdoor exercise which can benefit the whole family. It's fun! And as more people discover its competitive aspects, orienteering is becoming an exciting sport with enough demanding challenges to satisfy even the best of athletes. Moreover, it's a "thinking man's" sport.

Further, as more Americans take to the outdoors, orienteering takes on an added dimension—that of a necessary survival skill which any person going into the woods (or wilds) should have. Every person involved in outdoor activities which take them away from the traveled highways and byways should have a solid background in how to navigate with a map and compass; finding one's way should also be a basic skill for many outdoor sports. The uses for these skills are almost endless, but most important, just remember that orienteering is not only useful but fun.

## What Is Orienteering?

*Orienteering is the art of navigating through an unknown area using a map and compass as guide.* This activity can be a means to an end, or in the case of an orienteering competition, can be the end in itself.

Some view orienteering as merely a tool, a means by which one can find a fishing spot or remote picnic grounds—a way to find one's location in the woods or one's way. out. Hunters, fishermen, hikers, canoeists, bird watchers and others often have occasion to put the art of orienteering to good use, as we will see.

On the other hand, orienteering is also an organized sport which has long been popular in Europe and is now gaining popularity in the United States and Canada. Orienteering meets test both navigating ability and stamina as the contestants are timed as they "locate" themselves around various courses—courses usually set in a woodsy terrain. Before each meet the projected course is marked with "controls," or checkpoints, consisting of small red and white markers. These control points are then plotted on each contestant's map before he or she takes to the course: the object being to find and "punch-in" at all the controls faster than the other contestants do; rather like a sports car rally on foot, or a cross-country race without a prescribed course.

In the sports world, orienteering is closely related to others in the "environmental sports" family. Cross-country skiing, hiking and snow-shoeing are all close relatives. Orienteering also ties in well with sports that develop the cardiovascular system. Jogging, biking, hiking and swimming are all similar to orienteering in that they all act to develop the participants' hearts and lungs as well as their other muscles. And don't think that orienteering can be done only on foot; orienteering meets also take the shape of ski-orienteering, car-orienteering and scuba-orienteering.

### HOW TO START

Glad you asked! To learn about how to orienteer, for racing purposes or otherwise, read on . . . that's what this book is all

Young family enjoying a day on the orienteering trail.

about. You don't need loads of equipment, just a map and compass. You can learn by yourself or with others, but orienteering does not require a group of people. You can get started by yourself. Many people will choose to use the knowledge gained from this book without getting into the sport of orienteering. That's O.K. But those of you interested in trying your hand at competition, will find all you need to know about the techniques and rules for competition plus a section listing local orienteering clubs and some

of the established meets. Chances are there are now, or soon will
be, orienteering meets in your area. We have also included a
section on how you can start your own orienteering club.

## WHO CAN ORIENTEER?

Much more than for many sports, orienteering can be for everyone. People of all ages, abilities, and sexes can take part. One can
learn orienteering at one's own pace and choose one's own level
of involvement. We are not all racers; everyone is free to choose
orienteering for his or her own reasons.

*The Family.* A family may want to orienteer to have a low-cost
family outing. With only a map and compass—and armed with a
picnic lunch—any family can have an all-day, low-cost and pleasur-
able excursion. In the process, each member will get some good
exercise hiking, see some pretty country, have a chance to see some
birds and wildlife, plus the opportunity to enjoy being together
as a family. That's a lot of entertainment for the cost of a map
and compass.

*Sportsmen.* Sportsmen too can enjoy orienteering. Hunters will
feel more secure in the woods knowing where they are and how
to get home. Fishermen, as already noted, can re-locate that
favorite fishing hole. Bird watchers can leave the trails and paths
behind and get out into the more isolated areas where birds, not
people, abound. Hikers and other "outdoor" fanciers will relish the
joys of an afternoon in the woods. Orienteering even boasts a few
converts from motorcycle moto-cross events. Now they see the
back country under their own power.

*Competitors.* All ages can try their hand at competitive orienteering events patterned to test their varying abilities. Separate
courses are set covering a wide range of skill. There are almost
always beginner, intermediate and advanced courses to provide a
challenge to all attending. And the winners are not always the
swiftest of foot, but instead those who can read a map and use a
compass best. Stories abound of fast runners who have spent long

afternoons running about through the woods without ever locating all the control markers and never finishing. So, even if you're not a high-gear competitor and just want a sneaky way to get some good exercise, try orienteering.

First official use of the word "orienteering"—as shown on a winner's certificate at Oslo in 1900.

## History of Orienteering

Although orienteering is a recent sport in North America, it has a long history in other parts of the world—especially Scandinavia, where competitive orienteering was born. It seems to have evolved during the latter part of the 19th century from military exercises based on the idea of getting messages through unknown areas. These military events are documented from Stockholm, Sweden in 1893 and Bergen, Norway in 1897.

Interestingly enough it appears ski-orienteering started earlier than foot orienteering as a civilian sport—but not by much. On March 4, 1900 there was a relay (3-man?) ski-orienteering meet held between the Swedish towns of Bollnäs and Härnösand—a distance of 175 km (109 miles). Fighting their way through a bad blizzard, the winning team came in in a time of 28 hours and 27 minutes, or almost 4 miles an hour. What a start for a sport!

The same year, on October 7, the foot orienteers got their start at a meet organized by the club Tjalve in Oslo, Norway. At this event the word orienteering was used for the first time and was printed on the winner's certificate.

However, the early meets were very small affairs and continued to be so until after World War I. On March 25, 1919 the first breakthrough occurred—220 people showed up for a start. This meet, which was organized by Captain Ernst Killander, then president of the Amateur Athletic Association of Stockholm, is generally considered to be the birth of competitive orienteering. Recently a statue of an orienteer has been placed at the starting area of this first real race.

A GROWING SPORT

Since then orienteering has grown to a point that in Sweden, in the 1970's, it is, together with soccer, the most popular sport. There, at least 80,000 of the 8 million population are competitive orienteers. It is so much a national sport that it is a mandatory part of the school curriculum. Internationally, orienteering has reached at least 23 countries—the number of member countries of the International Orienteering Federation (IOF). These members come from quite different corners of the world, such as Australia, New Zealand, Japan, Israel, most European countries, and also Canada and the United States.

This growth came quite slowly and only after two equipment revolutions. The first of these occurred during the early 1930's when the Swedish Kjellström brothers, Björn and Alvar, together with Gunnar Tillander, developed the fast and simple one-piece protractor compass. This compass design is often also known as a Silva-type compass, after the name of the company the three top-

A fast finish at the 1975 5-day meet at Väster Haninge, Sweden.

level orienteers formed. The simplicity in operation of the new compass drastically widened the orienteering recruiting base—even 6- to 8-year-olds could learn how to use this compass.

The *second* major improvement in the sport came much later, in the 1960's, and more gradually. This time it concerned the maps, or rather how to make accurate maps. In order to be able to navigate his way precisely over a course, an orienteer wants all features and objects that he encounters along his route to be shown clearly on the map. No standard maps come close to that requirement. Frankly, very few common maps are accurate in regard to such obvious features as houses, fields, roads and paths. Often the information about these ever-changing details is outdated even before a map reaches the store.

So orienteers had to start making their own maps. Nobody but enthusiastic and *volunteer* orienteers could afford to do it. It's not unusual that a thousand hours of work go into a satisfactory map.

To produce a good orienteering map, orienteers must do most of the work—from plotting the aerial photos, to the field checking, to the actual artwork itself. Only orienteers know what details an orienteer wants and needs to see on the map he or she will use.

These new maps have narrowed the element of chance and have helped make orienteering both a precise and a fair sport in which only the best stand the best chance to win. Also, with the use of universal standards and symbols, it no longer much matters in what country or area a meet is held. This has made it possible for orienteering to become the true international sport that it is today.

### IN NORTH AMERICA

How did orienteering reach the North American continent? For one thing, Björn Kjellström moved to the United States where he has played a continuing role in the introduction and development of orienteering in both the United States and Canada. In

**Björn Kjellström—today and yesterday.**

1946 Kjellström made his first attempt to introduce orienteering. This first demonstration meet was run in the Indiana Dunes State Park and was followed in 1948 by races outside Montreal and Toronto. The meets did not continue for lack of enough enthusiastic leaders and organizers. However, undaunted, Björn continued to push the idea of orienteering in the form of map and compass exercises with youth groups such as the Scouts—though very little involvement spread outside these groups for some years.

Ski orienteering also got its North American start in 1948—at Turin, New York where it stayed alive and well for several years. Today, as we will see, it is enjoyed more or less regularly here and there as both a training exercise and an event. Ski orienteering, by the way, received Olympic status in 1949 at the Olympic Conference in Rome, but has never been included in any of the Games. Maybe at Lake Placid in 1980? Foot orienteering has not yet been classified an Olympic Sport.

*New Push in Canada.* It was not until 1965 that orienteering got a new push in North America. This time it came from England via the British orienteers Geoffrey Dyson and John Disley who introduced orienteering at the Canadian National Track and Field Coach's Clinic at Guelph, Ontario. The new sport was well received by the attending coaches and teachers and the program was extended the following years.

A key person in this development has been Alex "Sass" Peepre, a professor at the University of Guelph, and until his death recently, president of the Canadian Orienteering Federation. He realized the unique values of orienteering as a recreational sport and was one of the driving forces behind gaining recognition and support for the sport within the Canadian government. In 1967 the Ontario Orienteering Association was formed simultaneously with the Quebec O.A. In Quebec the sport's stronghold was in and around Montreal, supported strongly by Scandinavians living in that area. One of these was Harald Wibye, a seasoned Norwegian orienteer and the main proponent of the sport there.

In December 1967 a major step in the development of Canadian orienteering was taken with the establishment of the Canadian Orienteering Federation, and the following year the Canadians were able to stage their first Championship Meet in Gatineau Park near Ottawa.

*A Start in the U.S.* In the meantime, Harald Wibye had moved from Montreal and had settled in the Delaware Valley area. There, during a brief stay, he also managed to get orienteering pretty well established. At the same time, the U.S. Marine Corps Physical Fitness Academy in Quantico, Virginia became aware of the sport and initiated a program on orienteering for the Marines. These two places have both had meets on a continuous basis since 1967.

A Marine runner—at the 1975 New England championships.

The Marines, through their orienteering team, soon established themselves as the best orienteers in the United States. Interest in the new sport then picked up among other parts of the armed forces as well, especially within the Army. Its R.O.T.C. (Reserve Officers Training Corps) units were soon active in orienteering at many colleges and universities, helping to make the sport widely known.

Further progress in civilian orienteering came in 1970 at Southern Illinois University, with Andy Marcec, a professor at the university, as the prime mover. In October the university sponsored a meet labeled the "First U.S. Championships" near Carbondale, Illinois. However, a governing body for U.S. orienteering did not exist until August of 1971 when the United States Orienteering Federation (USOF) was formed.

THE STORY TODAY

Since these early years, orienteering has experienced a steady and considerable growth in both North American countries—as it should, being an environmentally sound sport in line with the thinking of many of today's concerned people—young and old. By the mid-1970's orienteering associations existed in all of Canada's provinces, supporting some 60 clubs with close to 2,000 orienteers. There the sport gets invaluable support from the Canadian government which considers orienteering to be a fitness activity suitable for everyone. This follows the line of thinking in many countries with socialized medicare—that it is wiser and cheaper to spend money on programs to help keep people away from hospitals rather than spend it on them after they become patients.

Today the younger U.S. Federation is not far behind in spite of no direct government aid. The USOF in 1975 had 1,500 members from over 40 clubs. These clubs, of which the majority are affiliated with various R.O.T.C. detachments, cover roughly half the states, with the highest density in the East. To date Canada has had the broadest span of orienteers covering all classes, but the United States has been very successful in the Men's Elite Class—thanks to the Armed Forces' orienteering teams (the reader should see the following chapter for a definition of the various orienteering classes).

In August, 1976 the biggest North American meet yet gathered more than 1,500 runners at the Quebec 5-day race. This turnout indicates that orienteering on this continent is growing toward becoming the mass participation sport that it is in many European countries, though admittedly there is still a ways to go to match the turnout at such impressive events as the O-Ringen 5-day meet in Sweden, with more than 10,000 participants, and the Swiss 5-day meet, with about half that number at the start lines. The O-Ringen is one of the world's biggest athletic events, with between 50,000 and 60,000 starts in the course of the meet.

SKI-O

Since its early beginnings in 1900 ski orienteering on its part has also developed into an international sport—though not to the same extent as foot orienteering. Many orienteering clubs and ski clubs across the snow belt of North America sponsor local ski-O events, and there are plans to organize meets on a more national level. With the current growth in cross-country skiing, ski-O is a natural addition and should soon gain considerable popularity.

This short look at the history of orienteering can only tell us where it has been. The future alone can tell us where it is going.

A CAPSULE HISTORY

The following is a list of the milestones in the development of orienteering:

1893   *Military Messenger competition in Stockholm, Sweden.*
1897   *Another Military Messenger competition outside Bergen, Norway.*
1900   *175 km Ski Orienteering Relay Competition between Bollnäs and Härnösand, Sweden.*
1900   *A civilian meet organized by the Club Tjalve of Oslo, Norway. The event was labeled as an "Orienteering Race" for the first time.*
1901   *Another civilian meet outside Sundbyberg, Sweden.*
1919   *A major breakthrough on March 25 at a meet outside Stockholm, Sweden when some 220 people participated.*
1932   *A team competition was held outside Oslo, Norway between Norway and Sweden.*

Obviously nothing daunted this 1928 Swedish competitor.

1935   The first National Championship organized in Sweden.
1937   Norway held National Championships, the second country to do so.
1938   Sweden became the first country to establish a National Orienteering Federation.
1938   Start of national team competition between Finland, Norway, and Sweden.
1942   Orienteering became a mandatory subject in Swedish schools.
1946   An Inter-Nordic Orienteering Organization formed.
1946   The first meet in the United States held at the Indiana Dunes State Park on the initiative of Björn Kjellström.
1947   The Nordic National Team Meet was extended to include Denmark.
1948   Ski orienteering started outside Turin, New York where it remained active for several years.
1948   Orienteering was introduced to Canadians outside Toronto and Montreal.
1948   Orienteering started in Switzerland, the first European country outside the Nordic block.
1949   Ski orienteering given Olympic Status at the Olympic Games Conference in Rome.

1957  Start of official Nordic Championships at Trondheim, Norway.

1961  The International Orienteering Federation (IOF) was formed in Copenhagen, Denmark by Bulgaria, BRD (West Germany), Czechoslovakia, Denmark, DDR (East Germany), Finland, Hungary, Norway, Sweden and Switzerland.

1962  The First European Championships were held in Löten, Norway.

1962  Orienteering introduced to Great Britain and Scottish Orienteering Association formed.

1965  Orienteering introduced at the Clinic for Track and Field Coaches at Guelph, Ontario.

1966  Start of World Championships at a meet at Fiskars, Finland. The meet is held every even year.

1967  The British Orienteering Federation formed.

1967  Provincial associations formed in Ontario and Quebec.

1967  Formation of the Canadian Orienteering Federation.

1967  Permanent orienteering groups formed in the U.S. located around the Delaware Valley and Quantico, Va.

1968  The First Canadian Championships held in Gatineau Park outside Ottawa.

1970  Southern Illinois University organized the First U.S. Championships.

1971  Founding of the United States Orienteering Federation (USOF).

1971  First North American Championships organized at Quantico, Va. The meet is held every odd year, alternately in Canada and the U.S.

1973  The O-Ringen 5-day meet in Sweden reached more than 10,000 participants, with runners from almost 30 countries.

1975  Ski orienteering World Championships in Finland.

1976  Quebec 5-day meet (in August) draws 1,500 entries.

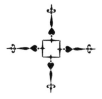

# The Event

THE BEST WAY to understand how orienteering works is to go to a meet. We can sit and talk, or read, about orienteering all day, but without actually venturing to an orienteering get-together it is hard to understand the true spirit of the sport. Since you probably can't jump up and get to a meet right this minute, let's look at a little of what a beginner's experience at a meet might be.

## Where to Go

Most orienteering meets are conducted in areas that are relatively free from man's traces. This does not mean that it must be a wilderness area, but orienteering requires space that has retained much of its natural qualities. A wooded area of 100 to 1,000 acres is ideal. Some man-made features—such as, fields, stone walls, logging roads, and hiking paths—scattered about the site actually enhance the land's value for orienteering. As a rule, the more obvious the features, the better the area is for beginners, and vice versa for experts.

Probably, the meet would be organized by a local orienteering club. Such clubs are composed of orienteering enthusiasts who not only participate in meets but also volunteer their time to conduct

A busy time at the meet secretary's desk—this time computing results.

meets as well. (See the appendix for a list of the active orienteering clubs in the United States and Canada.) These clubs have various ways to let you know when there will be a meet but we'll tell you more about that in the chapters on meet organization and publicity.

## A Sample Run

Come with us here on a fairly rudimentary tour of what happens when at an orienteering meet. More detailed information on the various events and necessary techniques will follow later.

Before you can start, there are a few preliminaries. Since orienteering meets attract a wide variety of people, most meets offer several different orienteering courses, each designed for people of different abilities. As a beginner, you couldn't be expected to tackle the same course as a seasoned veteran. In a minute, we'll get to what all the different courses and classes mean, but to get started on the right foot your first step should be to find the registration area. There, whoever is in charge of registration will likely ask you a few questions about your orienteering experience. Don't be afraid to say you're a beginner; probably most of the others at a meet will be newcomers too. Beginners are usually placed in the "wayfarer" course—a fairly simple course designed to give neophyte orienteerers a taste of the sport without too much involvement in compass and map-reading skills.

At the registration area you will be given the information needed for your course. *Maps of the area are given out; compasses are usually available for rent.* Along with the map, you will be given a "control card" which also serves as your score card.

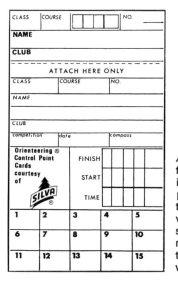

*A basic control card.* Note the fill-in spaces for all pertinent meet information: class, course, participant's name and number, starting time, etc. The bottom section travels with the competitor, the stub stays at the secretary's desk. The numbered boxes below indicate the proper punch points for the various controls.

Along with your control card, you will also be given a sheet of notices pertinent to the meet. Such a list would contain any corrections to be made on the map, any areas that are off-limits, and what time everybody should be out of the woods. Also essential is the control definition sheet. This is the code that tells you at what type of geographical feature you can expect to find the control you seek—the treasure of your hunt.

This is not the last you will see of the registration area. When you are ready you will return for your official starting time and again after the meet. This last is important: you must be sure to return to the finish (usually near the registration area) regardless of your performance. The officials check off the names of the finishers and, if you do not check in, the meet organizers must assume that you are still in the woods.

DON'T FOLLOW ME!
IM LOST TOO

Fortunately—this doesn't happen to many.

*What's a Control?* Here is as good a place as any to say a little more about what a control is. The controls are the specific spots—some would say pinpoints—on the course (as indicated on your master map) that are the goals of your orienteering. As we will see later, these can vary in number, shape, distance and difficulty but it is to these points that you direct your search—much as treasures in an old-fashioned treasure hunt.

If you have any questions about what you have to do after looking over the information and studying the map, this is the time to ask them and the registration desk is the place to do it. Meet directors and other enthusiasts always have a willing ear and some helpful words of advise for newcomers. Remember, once in the woods you're on your own, so now is the time to straighten out any problem. Orienteerers are a friendly lot, so don't be afraid to ask for help if you have forgotten all you should remember about contour lines from your Boy Scout days, or all you have learned about compasses—even after reading our *Map and Compass* chapter—becomes a foggy blur, or the rules seem confusing—or whatever.

### THE START

One of the joys of orienteering is that the meet starts when you are ready, not when the meet is ready. This is because every participant has his or her own starting time, to allow a staggered start—this to avoid congestion along the course. As a result, once you are on your way, you will probably see few of your competitors. As we have said it's mainly you and the woods.

The start at the O-Ringen meet in Sweden.

*Preparing Your Map.* Once you are ready to go, you are assigned a starting time, generally a few minutes away. This waiting period is a good time to get your thoughts collected. When the starter signals you to go, your first task is to proceed to the master-map area (usually a short distance away) to copy that day's course on your map. You'll notice right off how your orienteering map differs from the standard map you usually use but we'll talk more about that and what to do with it in *Map and Compass*. This copying of the control points to the map is a delicate operation which comes at a time when the adrenalin is flowing and you don't feel like doing paperwork. Nonetheless, drawing the course on your map should be done with great care. Once you're done, go back and check your work again for complete accuracy; a fraction of an inch misdrawn can mean a lot of extra hiking in the woods. A few extra seconds spent here can mean minutes, or sometimes even hours, in the woods. (This might be a good time to look at the fold-out map at the back of the book to see how the courses are drawn there.)

Occasionally, in championship meets, the area maps will have the courses predrawn for you. In which case, you receive your map at the start or shortly before and you're off. In either case, once you have a copy of your course and your compass, you are ready to orienteer. (This is becoming more common for beginner meets, too.)

The map is crucial to successful orienteering. The gal at left is copying her course from the master map; the gal at right carefully checking her course in the field.

### TO THE FIRST CONTROL

*Your Route Choice.* With all the red tape behind you, you're ready to begin the search for control #1. But before leaving the master-map area, closely scrutinize the choice of routes. What is the *easiest* way to the control? Chances are, the course setter has placed the first control of the wayfarer's course not too far away and at a fairly recognizable feature—and not requiring difficult compass work. Checking the map carefully, after a few moments of thought and with a game plan in mind, you're off, down the path which you chose as the best route. On your way, you must use your eyes as much as your legs, noticing every feature to see that it matches each feature as shown on the map.

*Approaching the Control.* Depending on how secure you are in your route choice, you may want to jog or run in the early stages, but as you approach the area of the control, slow down and refer to the map more closely so that you can cautiously feel your way to the marker. If all your calculations are right, the first control marker should be right over the next small knoll, ahead of you at the junction of your path and a stream. As you climb the knoll, the anxiety of whether you have navigated correctly is killing you. Nearing the top, you spot the stream on the other side and sure enough, there is that small red and white marker. What a great feeling! You did it! A quick inspection shows that this is the correct control (each control marker is keyed to match its counterpart on the map), so you whip out your score card and mark the proper box on the card with the punch hanging from the control. This, of course, is to attest to the fact that you found the proper control.

*At the control.* One youngster is obviously deciding his course to the next control, while the other is just approaching. Note the punch resting atop the crossbar.

ON TO #2

With a feeling of elation, you survey your choices of routes to control #2. After some thought, it appears your best route choice will include traveling part way on some paths, and then at a particular path junction taking—with the use of a compass—a bee-line of about 100 meters (approximately—for those of you not into the metric scene yet—100 yards) to the corner of the field where the marker is located. It won't take much experience to notice that the course setter has given you a choice: you could go the entire distance by paths, but that would be a roundabout way—or, you could go more directly through the bush. With your confidence brimming, you elect to do a bit of bush-wacking using the compass. Now you're catching on. The course setter purposely wanted to force you to make a choice. Now let's see if you have made the right choice. Well, congratulations, you came out of the woods right at the corner of the field and staring you in the face was marker #2. Good going! Now on to #3.

*But I thought it was easy . . .*

And so it goes to numbers 3 and 4. You attack each control point with the accuracy of a seasoned veteran and now only #5, the final control, remains. But wait a minute, the marker should be right here at this path intersection, and there is nothing here. There must be some mistake. Did the course setter misplace the marker? Or did you make an error? Chances are, it's you. Now where could you have gone wrong? Everything was going so smoothly, and this looked like the easiest of all the controls. Maybe you're getting tired. It seems like a good time to sit down and think, just as the meet director suggested for just such moments before you got started. Upon more careful inspection, the map reveals additional details—a boulder here, a small incline there —which, in your haste, you completely missed. In a few minutes of sitting you sort things out and establish your present position. After a little back-tracking, you approach the correct path junction and with it the marker. Your jog back to the finish presents no problem.

### THE FINISH

At the finish (generally, the same area as the start), you present your score card on which your time of finish is recorded and your elapsed time computed. Even though you didn't win, you experience a great feeling of satisfaction. You finished your course, even though you were temporarily lost; you mastered the woods. The day was exhilarating, the woods were beautiful, and without realizing it, you got a healthy dose of exercise. What more could you ask?

### THE POST MORTEMS

Probably one of the most enjoyable aspects of orienteering occurs after everyone is finished. Then, winners and losers alike, trade anecdotes and analyze their conquests and defeats of the day. The yarn-swapping sessions last almost as long as the race itself. Every competitor is convinced that, "my route to control #4 was the best," or, "that marker #5 was not properly placed at that boulder." Orienteerers are staunch individualists who do things their own way and the ensuing debates often border on the hilarious.

Now, with this brief introduction under your belt, read on for the finer points of the techniques involved and for the many other aspects of orienteering. Then, hopefully, there will soon be another meet, where with a little more skill and confidence—and a better understanding of what's involved—you can conquer a tougher course.

## Meet Structure

As mentioned at the beginning of this chapter, people of all ages and interests are attracted to orienteering meets. If all the participants were expected to knock off the same elite course in a meet, there would be a great many unable to find even a single control. Recognizing that people come in all sorts and sizes, orienteering meets offer several courses of varying length and difficulty. In this fashion, the meet provides a challenging event for everyone from elderly walkers and youngsters to charged-up runners. This situation is akin to the design of ski slopes. If a mountain offered only treacherous expert trails, few families would be attracted to its offerings. Consequently, as most ski areas contain a variety of trails varying from beginner to expert, so it is at orienteering meets with courses for people of all abilities.

COURSES — WHITE, YELLOW, RED, BLUE...

Orienteering courses are distinguished by an internationally recognized system of color codes. They vary from beginner, or "wayfarer," to expert. The accompanying chart shows the standard orienteering courses and the corresponding color code for each level of competition—White for beginner; Yellow for advanced beginner; Orange for intermediate; Red for advanced intermediate, and Blue for elite. (As shown in the appendix, some variation in color coding does exist from place to place and meet to meet.)

Areas of Difference. Notice that the courses differ not only by distance, but that the control placement becomes more sophisticated as the courses approach the expert level. As an example, most controls contained in a wayfarer course are located at a readily distinguishable feature, such as a corner of a field or a path junction; whereas on a more elite level, a control point might be a single boulder or small tree or bush.

| LEVEL OF DIFFICULTY | Beginner or "Wayfarer" | Advanced Beginner | Intermediate | Advanced Intermediate | Elite or Expert |
|---|---|---|---|---|---|
| COURSE COLOR | WHITE | YELLOW | ORANGE | RED | BLUE |
| Classes Commonly Using the Course | Novice Men and Women. | Boys and Girls (14 years and under). Recreation classes of all ages. | Girls (15 to 18 years) Men (50 and up). Women (35 and up). | Elite Women (19 years and up) Men (35 and up) Boys (15 to 20) | Elite Senior Men (21 years and up). |
| Average Length of Course | Up to 3 Km* | 3½ to 4¼ Km | 3¼ to 4¼ Km | 5 to 7 Km | 7 to 12 Km |
| Average Number of Controls | 4 to 8 | 6 to 8 | 6 to 8 | 6 to 10 | 8 to 15 |
| Difficulty of Control Placement | Easy, obvious locations, near paths and roads. | Near large map features, less obvious than white course. | Varied difficulty; some in remote locations, some fairly accessible. | Difficult locations along long legs between controls. | Difficult locations, low to ground, at small map features. |
| Orienteering Skills Needed to Complete Course | Basic map reading, some compass bearing skills. | More precise map reading and compass use. | Pace counting, good map reading, rough and precision compass. | All | All |
| Winner's Approximate Time | 30 to 40 min. | 40 min. | 50 min. | 60 min. | 60 to 80 min. |

*Km, or kilometer, equals 0.62137 miles.

So, the moral of the story is don't tackle something over your head. Regardless of your physical condition, take the time to navigate a White course on your first orienteering outing. If you breeze through it like a piece of cake, there is always time to move up to a Yellow or Orange course later in the day. Initial success is good for one's ego which inevitably will become sufficiently bruised before too long. Some capable orienteers never leave the White course level and are perfectly happy in so doing. That's fine. One of the great joys of orienteering is that everyone can do his own thing. There is room for everyone.

This is perhaps a good time to take another look back at the fold-out map—for a more graphic idea of just how orienteering courses work. The beginner and elite courses there will give you a better understanding of the obstacles to be met in these categories.

A runner approaching an elite course marker. The marker placement, low and slightly behind the boulder, is just right for this degree of difficulty.

CLASSES

Just as there are various courses to challenge the various competitors, there are different classes in which to record their results. These are based on the competitor's age, sex and experience in orienteering. To date, in most meets, a person voluntarily places himself or herself in the class they desire, but if orienteering continues to grow in this country as it has in Europe, class placement will probably be mandatory, based on previous performance.

Once again, as we saw with the standard course descriptions, an international code prevails for the various class titles. All men's classes are titled with an "H" for the German "Herren"; the female classes "D" for "Damen." Let's look at an example:

H 19-A

The H means that it is a men's class. The number in the middle always signifies the minimum age of the competitor. Thus everyone in this class must be at least 19 years old. The final initial stands for the level of competition in the class; "A" being the best or elite level. "B" and "C" categories indicate lower levels of competition, much like the classification for ski races. Thus, H 19 B competitors would be men over 19 who, because of their skills and/or interests, chose to run an easier course. Sound complicated? Don't worry about it. The only reason for the entire system is so that you can measure your performance against other competitors of like age, sex, interests, and skills. This system allows many winners at each meet to be recognized as tops in their level of competition. Hopefully, this will encourage people of all ages and both sexes to try orienteering.

Incidentally, all orienteering meets are open to both men and women. Women have true equality in this sport. Orienteering is also leading the way on the issue of amateurism. Since the beginning of organized international orienteering, there has been no distinction made between the professional or the amateur competitor. All orienteers compete together.

It should be mentioned that if you go to a small local orienteering meet, you probably won't be faced with this bewildering maze of classes. If fewer than 50 participants are expected, the meet director usually sets just two or three courses, with a men's and ladies' division. As we said earlier, if you are in doubt as to where you belong, let the person who registers you decide. He or she will have a good idea of what the courses are like and can put you in the right spot. One final hint: even if no longer a rank beginner, in your early meets always start a little below where you think you might belong. A too discouraging outing could mark the end of what could be a lifelong career of happy orienteering.

## Types of Events

Now that you've got the basic idea of the game, we should explain that there are several types of orienteering meets. Almost all the meets conducted in this country, as well as internationally, are called cross-country orienteerings. Because it is the most popular form of the sport, cross-country has become almost synonymous with the name orienteering. But there are other forms of orienteering events. Read on.

CROSS-COUNTRY ORIENTEERING

This is the type of event we described at the outset of this chapter. All championship meets, and in fact all international competition, follow this format. All competitors must visit all the controls on their respective courses in the prescribed order. Cross-country orienteering is considered the purest form of the sport.

SCORE ORIENTEERING

This is an intriguing variation of the basic cross-country orienteering format. The meet organizer places a larger number of controls, perhaps 12 to 20, in areas of varying difficulty. Each control is assigned a point value between 5 and 30, depending on its difficulty. In this case, the course map would indicate the point value as well as the control location. A control located near the start and at an easily recognized feature would have a low value. As the controls move further away from the start or are placed by hard-to-find features, their relative value goes up.

The purpose of this event is to tally as many points as possible by locating the maximum number of high-valued controls within an allotted time period. There is no set order for finding the controls and each person must determine the optimum way to use his or her allotted time, keeping in mind his own endurance and skill. It's a great game, after which there is endless discussion as to what was the best order to collect the controls for the highest score. Our club uses this type of meet when there is a limited amount of time available, such as in the middle of the week. Score orienteering offers several advantages:

1. You can be sure that all the competitors will be back before dark. A penalty is usually subtracted from a person's score if they exceed the time limit.

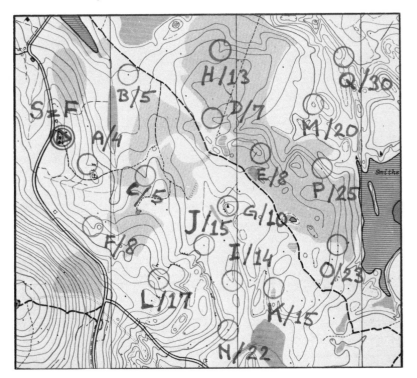

*A sample score orienteering course.* This event tests a wide range of orienteering skills—sound, quick judgment above all perhaps. But it also allows a good bit of freewheeling—a nice bonus on occasion. A penalty of 3 points is subtracted from the competitor's score for each minute in excess of the 60-minute allotted time. *Remember:* for a full list of control symbols while working with these maps, see the appendix and fold-out map.

Start: The field
Control/Points

| | |
|---|---|
| A/4: | The re-entrant |
| B/5: | The boulder (1½ m), south side |
| C/5: | The re-entrant |
| D/7: | The re-entrant, upper end |
| E/8: | The ridge, southeast part |
| F/8: | The re-entrant, lower end |
| G/10: | The hut |
| H/13: | The re-entrant, upper end |

| | |
|---|---|
| I/14: | The ridge, south part |
| J/15: | The knoll, south foot |
| K/15: | The marsh, north edge |
| L/17: | The cliff foot (2 m) |
| M/20: | The depression |
| N/22: | The boulder (1 m), west side |
| O/23: | The boulder (1½ m), north side |
| P/25: | The boulder (1 m), east side |
| Q/30: | The pit (ø 3 m) |

Finish: The field
Allotted time: 60 min.

2. The participators left standing around after a meet can help the organizer pick up the markers.

3. It encourages the orienteer to use his time wisely and to work under pressure.

4. Due to the time limit, the competitor runs a little faster than usual—a great early-season conditioner.

TRIM ORIENTEERING

This is a new form of orienteering which has a lot to offer in the way of recreation. Basically, it's the same game as score orienteering, but without the time limit. 50 to 100 controls are placed in the woods on a semipermanent basis. Maps are made showing the position of the controls and distributed to as many people as possible. The controls are then left in the woods for an extended period allowing all comers to try to find as many markers as possible. Since this time period could be from one month to half a year, ordinary orienteering markers won't do, but small, colorfully painted markers of wood or aluminum work well.

*The advantages and uses of such a course are many.* Families can learn the art of orienteering together and at their own pace. People can use the course at their convenience because it's always there. School groups can use the course for an instructional area. Trim orienteering very nicely accomplishes the main goal of orienteering—to get people outdoors to exercise and to have fun.

It is the responsibility of the organizer to promote the course and distribute the maps. Sporting goods stores and conservation groups can serve as distribution centers. Local newspapers and radio stations can help with publicity.

By charging a small fee for each map or score card, the person or group organizing the course can raise some money. Local orienteering clubs could use the proceeds towards the printing of improved maps or the purchase of orienteering equipment. Awards could be mailed to the family or person finding the most controls.

Obviously, if the land is not club-owned (or privately, by an agreeable host), permission must be sought to set up such a course;

but local and state authorities are often cooperative. And such a course on a semipermanent basis is certainly worth the effort.

## RELAY ORIENTEERING

As a variation of cross-country orienteering, a relay race can provide considerable extra excitement. Similar to other relay races, an orienteering relay places a premium on the combined efforts of several average performers, rather than on one outstanding competitor—giving the little guy a chance to share the spotlight. In the United States and Canada relays are usually held in conjunction with a championship meet, generally scheduled the day previous to the running of the major event. In Scandinavia, on the other hand, relay races are among the most prominent events, often standing on their own. The "Tiomila" relay in Sweden is one of the biggest sporting events of the year and features 300-plus club teams, each consisting of ten men. The event begins late in the afternoon and continues through the night with the winners finishing early the next morning. As you can imagine, the organizational effort required for that meet is immense. But, with the help of an army of workers, the event runs very smoothly.

*How It Works.* The Tiomila is an example of a "clover leaf" relay—the most popular variety of orienteering relay racing. Each leg of the clover leaf fans out in different directions from a central start and finish area, much like spokes of a wheel from a hub.

The start is staggered of course so that the competitors cannot simply follow one another around the course.

To keep the competition moving, there is usually a maximum of two hours allowed for each competitor, or leg: After the allotted time has elapsed, the next runner is often permitted to begin even if his teammate has not returned from the previous leg. Such an arrangement gives the teammates on the later legs some incentive, with the competition still within reasonable bounds.

In keeping with the spirit of orienteering, mixed relays are always fun and family relay teams also add spice to a meet. Just specify which legs are for the ladies or kids, and keep all legs within reach of most people's abilities.

## NIGHT ORIENTEERING

Now here's a challenge for those who think they have map and compass handling firmly in hand. Night orienteering is a humbling experience but an exhilarating one. Only a few night events have been held in North America, but the results have been encouraging. Hopefully, this aspect of the sport will also grow.

There are some modifications to the basic cross-country orienteering format which must be made before even seasoned competitors can be sent out into the dead of night. Here's a good model to follow:

1. Select an area that is relatively civilized. Athletic complexes and municipal parks make good sites.

2. Place controls at readily distinguishable features. Many good control points for day meets become too difficult to locate at night, so put the markers at noticeable features such as path junctions, corners of buildings and the like.

3. Shorten the distance for the event. A length of 3 to 4 kilometers for senior men should provide a suitable challenge, with correspondingly shorter courses for juniors and ladies.

4. Place a red lantern or small light source of some sort inside the markers so that the control can be seen from a distance.

5. Be doubly sure that everyone checks in at the finish regardless of whether they complete the course or not.

If you plan on competing in a night orienteering meet, you will need more than just the standard orienteering equipment outlined in the following chapters—map, compass, footgear and such. A head lamp such as those used by spelunkers and night cross-country skiers is required equipment, and a couple of extra bulbs in your pocket aren't a bad idea either. A whistle is also a good item to have—just in case you get way off track. Also remember that it gets cool at night and that you won't be traveling as fast as during the day. An extra layer or two of clothes will solve this problem.

Above all, a good dose of common sense must prevail at such meets, both on the part of the meet organizer and the contestants. The area selected by the organizer must be devoid of any dangerous

This orienteer is combining night and ski orienteering—not meant for beginners. Note the wristband compass and headlamp.

features. Cliffs, deep rivers and busy highways do not belong in night orienteering. The controls should be reasonably placed allowing most people a chance to find them without becoming hopelessly lost. And once again, you shouldn't try night orienteering if you are a neophyte to the sport. Hone your skills at least at a few day events before you take to the woods at night—nobody likes to go back out on a rescue mission after finishing a race late at night.

## ASSIGNMENT ORIENTEERING

Particularly suitable for summer camps, Boy Scout outings and other outdoor education programs, assignment orienteering offers an interesting twist to the basic theme. Its main point of difference is that once a contestant, or group of contestants, arrive at a control, they find an assignment or project to do at that spot. We have seen some imaginative projects pursued in this fashion—projects often designed to tie other outdoor skills in with orienteering. Such a task might be to identify various trees or flowers in the immediate vicinity of the control, or to start a fire without matches, or to tie some particular knots. Some controls for assignment orienteering must necessarily be manned and others might just require written instructions, with some arrangement suggested for proof of accomplishment. This form of orienteering can be used quite effectively whenever a new challenge is needed to spice up an outdoor education program.

## Variations of Orienteering

As you probably realize by now, orienteering does not have to be limited to just foot power. There are a number of rewarding variations to this basic method of travel. Once again, people are limited only by their imagination as to how to use orienteering. The only immutable factor should be that, in keeping with the spirit of orienteering, the sport should always remain compatible with the environment that it uses. The purpose of orienteering is to entice people to get out to appreciate and use the out-of-doors. But destroying the land does not make sense. So, let's forget about snowmobile and motorcycle orienteering right away. However, here are some viable, healthy alternatives:

### SKI ORIENTEERING

The most popular variation of orienteering is ski orienteering, or ski-O, as many call it. The probable reason for this is the logical combination of two closely related sports. Many orienteers are cross-country skiers in the winter and vice versa. This is especially true in Scandinavia.

Ski orienteering differs from foot orienteering basically in the positioning of the controls. Whereas in dry-land orienteering, the control may be tucked away in a difficult spot, in ski orienteering, the controls are usually readily accessible from paths, with the difficult part being the route choice. Since such a premium is placed on route choice, it is the responsibility of the meet organizer to set the course so that there are several routes from one control to the next. Map reading and route choice, as well as skiing ability, are the name of the game.

Over the past winters, a few ski-O events have been held in New England. The Ski Touring Council and the Eastern Ski Association (E.S.A.) are both interested in the recreational value

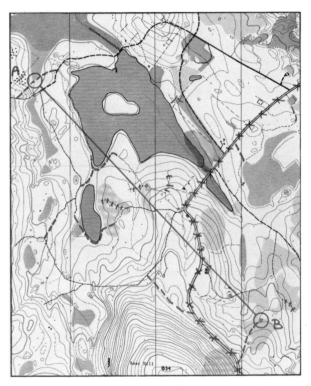

*A typical ski-O leg.* Long legs with easy controls accessible by trails are required for ski orienteering. Route choice is the key to ski-O. Alternate routes are offered by showing ski or snowmobile tracks on the map as well. Non-skiable trails and roads are also shown. A ski-O course is usually twice as long as a corresponding foot-orienteering course. Obviously, the idea is to get from A to B as quickly as possible.

*Map correction symbols used:*
*Ski or snowmobile track:*  — — — — — — — —
*Sanded or snow-free road or trail:*  ✕ ✕ ✕ ✕ ✕ ✕ ✕ ✕
*Over-snowed trails or roads:*  ⌠ ⌠ ⌠ ⌠ ⌠ ⌠ ⌠ ⌠ ⌠ ⌠
*(All trails and roads shown and not marked "over-snowed" must be pass-able.)*

of the sport. Perhaps with a good fall of snow and some eager orienteers, more skiers can be persuaded to try this sport.

## CANOE ORIENTEERING

Have you ever been on a canoe trip when you were the one responsible for finding the beginning of portage trails? It's not an easy task to locate the narrow trail head from the middle of a lake, is it? Well, canoe orienteering is basically the same game. Controls are placed at various points along the shore for the paddlers to locate. Prominent features such as peninsulas, islands and marshes make good control points.

This is another natural activity for campers and Scouts. Obviously, safety factors must be considered.

## BICYCLE ORIENTEERING

This can be another natural combination of two recreational pastimes. Everywhere you go these days, you find 10-speed bikes. Why not test the bikers' map-reading skills by staging a bike orienteering meet in your area? It's not hard. In fact, we have 4 or 5 such events around suburban Boston every year. You need an area that contains 10 to 20 miles of relatively traffic-free back roads and an up-to-date road map of the area. No topographical maps are needed here, although they sometimes can help. Controls can be water-painted (for easy removal later) on the roadside and no off-road cycling should be required. As in ski orienteering, the role of route choice is the big one. A good bike orienteering course allows 2 to 4 good alternative routes between controls. In this fashion, the cyclists' navigation skills are tested as much as their legs.

## OTHERS

These in no way represent a definitive list of all the types of orienteering. There are certainly others. Maybe you can dream up some of your own. How about sailing orienteering? Inner-city orienteering? Snowshoe orienteering?

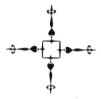

# Map &
# Compass

An ESPECIALLY ATTRACTIVE feature of orienteering is its simplicity. There is no expensive equipment required, and once you shell out the small initial outlay, there are few—if any—operating costs, such as lift tickets or greens fees. There are no yearly changes in compass models to keep up with and the sport is pretty nearly devoid of fancy paraphernalia. Further, what little there is is in no way essential. But there are some necessary pieces of equipment and the following are good guidelines to bear in mind:

1. Orienteering equipment should be functional. Buy equipment that is consistent with your needs. For example, if you are going to be a walker at an occasional local orienteering meet, there is no need to purchase the special lightweight orienteering shoes that many of the veteran orienteers prefer.

2. Don't cut corners on the one or two key items that are required. For instance, the compass is of paramount importance to an orienteer. It just doesn't make sense to try your first orienteering meet with a small compass from a Cracker Jack box. Good quality equipment more than pays off for the few items that the sport requires.

In this chapter, we will deal with the two essential pieces of equipment for all orienteers—the map and compass. In the following chapter you will find information on the other, more personal gear.

# The Map

The orienteer without his map is like a duck out of water. Maybe you'll want to think of the map as a book (hopefully of the non-fiction variety)—a book with a language all its own and which, when of good quality, can offer a wealth of vital information. It is the orienteer's task to gleen that information from the map. As we have seen, at organized orienteering meets proper maps will be provided. But let's look a little more at what a "proper" map should be.

### WHICH MAP?

Orienteering is done with a specific type of map—a topographical map, sometimes referred to as a "topo" map. As we will see, this map differs from a road map in several aspects. And, strictly speaking, the especially prepared orienteering map varies somewhat from the everyday topo map, as we will see.

In the United States, topo maps are prepared by the United States Geological Survey (U.S.G.S.) and are available at sporting goods stores, hiking and camping stores, and sometimes at book stores. If you get stuck and can't locate such a store, drop a post-card to:

>   National Cartographic Information Center
>   507 National Center
>   Reston, VA 22092

They will send an index of available maps from which you can locate the ones you need. The maps cost approximately $1.00 apiece.

In Canada topographical maps are made by the Department of Mines and Technical Surveys, located in Ottawa. A postcard to them will get you their index as well. Write to:

>   Map Distribution Office
>   615 Booth Street
>   Ottawa, Ontario K2E 6N4

BASIC MAP INFORMATION

If we view the map as a book, what are some of its chapters? Should you not have a topo map handy, you might want to refer to the especially prepared orienteering fold-out map at the back of the book as we go along.

*Location.* When you look at a topo map, notice the title of the map in large letters in both the top right and bottom right margins. The title is derived from the central feature of the particular area, usually a town.

*Date.* In the bottom margin you will find the date of that particular edition of the map. Both man-made (*i.e.*, house sites) and natural features (*i.e.*, forests) can change their form rather rapidly. Many maps now in use were made in the 1930's and 1940's and therefore lack many of the more recent feature changes. Keep this in mind while using the map.

*Scale.* Centered at the middle of the bottom margin, directly below the map, is the scale, stated in the form of a ratio. In the United States, topo maps are made in one or the other of two usable scales: 1:24,000 or 1:62,500. What do all these numbers mean? Simple! If it is a 1:24,000 map, it means that one unit of measurement on the map represents 24,000 of that same unit on the face of the earth. For instance, one foot on the map would equal 24,000 feet of distance on the land; one inch would equal 2,000 feet or a little over ⅓ mile. The same goes for 1:62,500; in this case an inch equals very nearly a mile. Thus, by using the map's scale, we can determine the distances the map represents. For orienteers this means we can figure pretty accurately the distances we have to travel. To help us further, most map makers include some common distances in scale in the bottom margin.

In Canada, the scales commonly used for topographical maps are 1:25,000 and 1:50,000.

## Sound confusing? . . .

Using the fold-out map supplied at the back of this book, or a favorite of your own choice—or better yet several maps of varying scale—test yourself a bit on this matter of map scale and distance determination. It's good practice for the real thing. Choose two points at a reasonable distance from each other on the map. Measure the exact distance to be covered on the map, then consult the map's scale, to see how far that distance would be on the earth's surface. Then, drawing on your memory bank, try to project just how much traveling distance that represents. After some practice, you will develop an "eye" for scale. As hardly needs to be said, orienteers prefer the 1:24,000-scale maps over the 1:62,000 for their added accuracy. In fact, some meet promoters blow the maps up even more for added detail—sometimes to a scale as large as 1:10,000. A case in point is the fold-out map herewith, in a scale of 1:15,0000.

*Which Way Is North?*   All topographical maps are laid out with North—true North, that is—at the top of the map, making the right margin the easterly border and so on around. Keep in mind two things: one, that the side borders of the map run North/South; and two, that your compass needle will follow a different North— magnetic North. Confused? (*magnetic* North is the northerly point towards which the meridians between the two magnetic poles are drawn.) To meet this discrepancy, most experienced orienteers draw magnetic-North lines on any standard maps they are to use, while most specially prepared orienteering maps show the magnetic-North lines (commonly called meridians) already drawn. However, don't linger over this small discrepancy between norths—just remember that the top of the map is North. We'll handle the compass's North later.

*Elevation.* One of the distinguishing features of a topographical map is its presentation of elevation in terms of given feet above sea level. How do map makers measure this? That's complicated and not important. What is important is that you learn how to read the map to determine the change in elevation.

If you will look at your topo map, you will notice many squiggly brown lines running all over. If you look closer, you will notice that they don't run in random fashion, but in a pattern. The lines form circles which are concentric, or in other words, ringed around each other like waves from a stone thrown into a pond. These brown lines are called contour lines and represent a certain change in elevation between them. Exactly how much change of elevation is told in the bottom margin of the map under the heading "contour interval." If the contour interval of a map is indicated as 10 feet, that means that there is a change or a difference of 10 feet in elevation between each contour line. For a better picture of contour lines, see the two-page spread following.

Now the hard part: notice that we called the distance between contour lines a "difference in elevation," but that we didn't tell you if the difference was a rise or a drop. Here is where you must look at the map closely. Remember, we said that the circles were concentric, or inside one another, right? Well, the innermost or smallest circles are the highest elevations, usually mountains or hill tops, and as the circles expand, the elevation drops off. Sometimes this gets confusing, but there is no easy way to decipher contours other than by careful scrutiny. However, there are some helpful clues to keep an eye out for while reading contours. For instance, if you are near a stream or river (note that rivers and streams on your topo map are indicated by a thin blue line), that usually signifies a low point relative to the remaining area in its

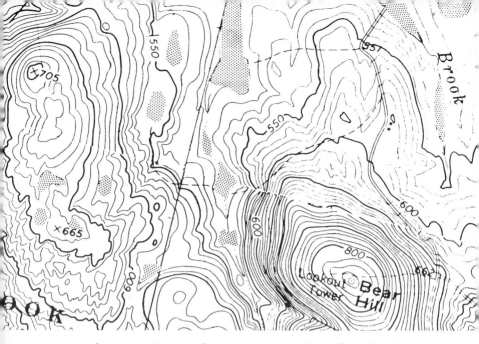

general vicinity. As a result most contours along the sides of a river (or most any body of water) represent a climb in elevation. (There is a good example of this in the upper left-hand corner of the fold-out map.) Likewise, with swamps and marshes. If you spend a little practice time with a topo map, you will soon become very sensitive to contour lines—they are invaluable aids to navigation.

*Map Symbols and Terms.* At the beginning of this chapter, we likened the map to a book and hinted that, if you hope to be able to read this book, you must learn the language. This language is comprised of terms such as the "contour interval" we have just discussed and a rather extensive variety of map symbols. Unlike a foreign language, this one is easy to learn and is based chiefly on plain common sense. Almost everything of significance seen on the landscape has a symbol in this map language. It won't take you long to identify many of the man-made and natural features shown. What does a cemetery look like on a map? A cross surrounded by a dotted line marking its borders. Makes sense. A well, on the other hand, is indicated by a small light-blue circle, while a rather comb-like symbol marks a cliff. To give you a better understanding of map symbols and what they represent, a glossary of symbols is included in the appendix, and a fairly complete legend is given on the fold-out map.

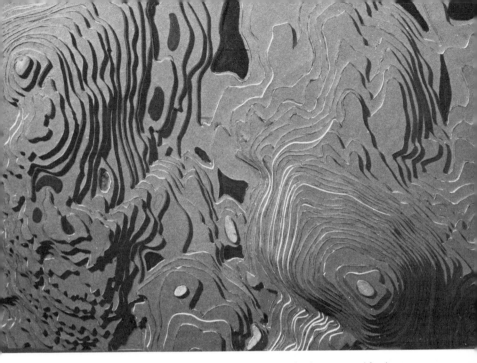

*Understanding maps. At left:* a section of a standard topographical map not yet adjusted for orienteering. *At right:* a bird's-eye and eye-level view of the same section of terrain, taken from a specially prepared diorama. This interesting juxtaposition—despite some slight distortion in the diorama and the absence of intervening brush—allows the orienteer to see how the elevations and other natural features suggested on the map translate in the field. As we shall see, an official orienteering map—in either black and white or color—would offer considerably more help: it would show more subtle differentiation in terrain and a greater abundance of features—both natural and man-made.

Just a word about the accuracy of maps. Remember, maps are a symbolic presentation of a small section of the earth's surface. To include all the features that exist on that area in their infinite complexity, would be an impossible task. Also, bear in mind that maps are made by men—mortals all, and prone to make an occasional mistake.

Before you have had much experience orienteering, you will discover some of these inaccuracies and/or omissions, but it is all part of the game. Learn to look at the map with a discerning eye. As we have said, our present system of topo maps was not designed with orienteering in mind; furthermore, many of these Geodetic Survey maps are very outdated. So, bear this in mind as you take on the woods.

SPECIAL MAPS FOR O

With the advent of orienteering as a sport, a new type of map designed expressly for orienteering has emerged. In the United States such maps for maybe two dozen good orienteering areas exist—areas with lots of interesting features and a lack of civilization, etc. Hopefully, as the sport grows, more orienteering maps will appear. Canada is way ahead of the United States; orienteerers there having made at least twice as many of these maps.

An orienteering map is based on the topographical map for a particular area, but refined and detailed to make navigation on foot accurate and more enjoyable. For instance, the scale for orienteering maps generally varies from 1:10,000 to 1:20,000 which makes possible for greater detail of a given area (as we have noted, the scale for the fold-out map with *Orienteering for Sport and Pleasure* is 1:15,000). Contour lines are more precise having been drawn from new aerial photos. Finally, the area is field-checked by an orienteer or a group of orienteers to include many details of the geography which an average cartographer would ignore. Cliffs, large boulders, intermittent stream beds and small paths are added, giving the orienteer much more data with which to navigate. Orienteering with such maps is sheer joy and allows the participant to move quickly and accurately and in large measure reduces the element of luck in the results of orienteering meets. These maps are generally shown in three or four colors on a 8″ x 11″ sheet. As a result of this very particular interest in special maps, it is understandable that everywhere orienteering becomes popular, among those attracted to the sport are map-makers. These folks just love to correct existing maps and to produce beautiful, accurate orienteering maps and couldn't care less about the races that are held using them. Their quest is an accurate map and the satisfaction of seeing people enjoy the results of their toil.

## USING THE MAP

Without dwelling here on the various precise techniques of orienteering—that comes later, here are a few hints about using your map as you attempt to navigate.

1. *Look at the map closely before you take a step.* First determine the general outline of the course you must follow from the control points indicated on the map you have copied or have been given. (For the purposes of our discussion here, you might want to turn to the beginner's course outlined on the fold-out map at the back of the book.) Then, examine what lies ahead along your path. What natural features are there to go by? What landmarks should be obvious? Will the terrain be rising or falling as you travel? What is the distance to the first control? These are all questions that you should ask yourself before you move.

2. *Orient your map to match the land.* Unlike a book which must be read from top to bottom and left to right, a map can be read in any position. To make things easier for you, turn the map to coincide with the direction of the land. For example, if you are going to travel in a westerly direction, with the map flat in front of you turn it so that the westerly border is at the top and facing geographic West. Now you, the map, and the land are all working together. As you travel West, features will appear on the map in the same order and placement as they do on the land. As you turn, adjust the map so that it is still aligned correctly. This is called orienting your map—thus, the word "orienteering." After a

You'll note that the young lady so intently studying her map has folded it carefully in a plastic case that is both flexible and protective (see below).

while, you will learn to do this naturally and make corrections of your map's position without thinking as you go along.

3. *Fold your map to a workable size.* Your map is your guide when you are in the woods, and you can't afford to lose or damage it. To prevent it from getting knocked around by branches and bushes, as well as to make it easier to work with, fold the map so that only the part you are using is visible. If you are using a map case (which you should), the folds will not be permanent and you can make any necessary adjustment at each control point. Folding the map and holding it as shown in the accompanying picture, you will be able to keep close tabs on your progress.

It has often been said "A good orienteer knows where he is, even when he's lost." Sound contradictory? Not really—good orienteers can figure out where they are even if they get off their track. How do they do it? By reading their maps super-carefully and by continually noting their progress.

## The Compass

The compass is second only to the map among the orienteer's most important tools. It is mainly used to aid you in keeping as straight a course as possible from one feature to another, for example when you cross through a wooded area or guide yourself from a known point to a hidden control.

### COMPASS CONSTRUCTION

The compass type most frequently used in orienteering is the protractor compass, more commonly known as a Silva-type compass after the company that first devised the idea of permanently attaching the protractor to the compass. This innovative construction makes it easy to take a compass bearing directly from the map as we will see later.

This compass type consists of two basic parts that in most compasses are found separated:

1. **The base plate** (*the protractor*)—made of a transparent material and normally with various scales along its edges; e.g., measuring scales in centimeters or millimeters. (A favorite orienteering compass, much as the compass shown in the following diagram, is limited to one measuring edge and has extra interchangeable scales available to slide over this edge as needed to concur with the scale of the map being used.)

2. **The compass housing**—mounted on the base plate in a way so it can easily be rotated. The bottom of the housing is, in most cases, transparent.

On the compass shown the names of the compass parts are spelled out. The basic ones are:

1. *Direction-of-travel* arrow. This, together with the *auxiliary direction lines*, and the longer edges of the base plate are all *direction lines*. (Also sometimes known more simply as the *direction arrow*.)

2. *North arrow*. This is the arrow etched into the bottom of the turnable compass housing. You will also note several auxiliary lines

# The Parts of
# a Compass

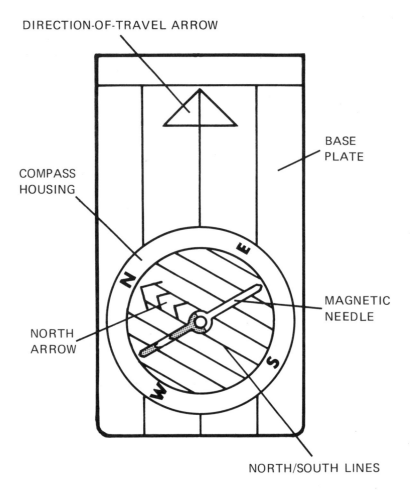

DIRECTION-OF-TRAVEL ARROW

BASE
PLATE

COMPASS
HOUSING

MAGNETIC
NEEDLE

NORTH
ARROW

NORTH/SOUTH LINES

parallel to the *North arrow*. They are all known as the *North/ South lines*.

3. *Magnetic needle*. The suspended needle whose red end always points North (if you don't use the compass close to iron objects). The needle is freely mounted in the compass housing which is filled with oil, the oil to slow down and dampen the needle's movement.

Although not shown on the diagram, a *carrying strap* is an important addition to the orienteering compass. Usually made of heavy twine, this strap offers the orienteer good protection from losing the compass; for example, at a fall. (The best way to arrange this strap is to tie a slip knot on the strap so the end of the strap forms a relatively small loop. Pull this loop over your preferred hand and tighten it loosely around your wrist with the slip knot. Using the strap this way gives you all possible flexibility— and, with the compass held lightly in your hand, allows you to check your bearing even while running, still secure in the knowledge that the compass won't fall free should you drop it.)

Study the diagram closely to be sure you have all the parts clearly in mind—and double check yourself by locating them all on the various compasses shown in the compass collection photo as well.

## USING THE COMPASS

The orienteer uses his compass for several important purposes. Let's look at the four basic ones: 1) *taking a compass bearing;* 2) *running on a bearing;* 3) *setting the map,* and 4) *determining position.*

*Taking a Compass Bearing.* This is a *three-step procedure* that can easily be learned. Most often it is learned mechanically, but there is also a logical explanation, as we will see later. Each of the three steps must be performed carefully because there is one pitfall to avoid in each step. If you don't avoid them you might end up going in the opposite direction from the one intended. Remember —you can use the fold-out map to practice with.

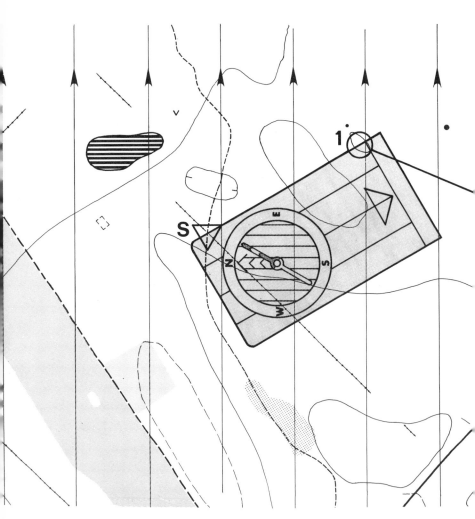

*Setting direction.*

*Step* 1.  Setting your direction. One possible route from S (the start and your present location) to 1 (the first control and your destination) is along a straight compass course. To set this course, place the longer edge of the compass's base plate, or one of the other *direction lines*, on the map along the line of intended travel. Or in other words, have a *direction line* go over both your present location and your destination. **Watch out:** Be sure that the *direction-of-travel* arrow is pointing from your location to your destination.

*Step 2.* Setting the *North/South lines.* With the compass base plate pressed firmly against the map to prevent the compass from moving, turn the compass housing around until the *North/South lines* in its bottom are parallel to the map's North lines (remember, we said earlier that most orienteering maps will have the North lines drawn in and that you should draw them in if they aren't) and with the *North* arrow (not the *needle*) pointing to the North of the map. **Watch out:** Be sure that the *North* arrow in the compass housing points to North on the map.

*Setting the North/South lines.*

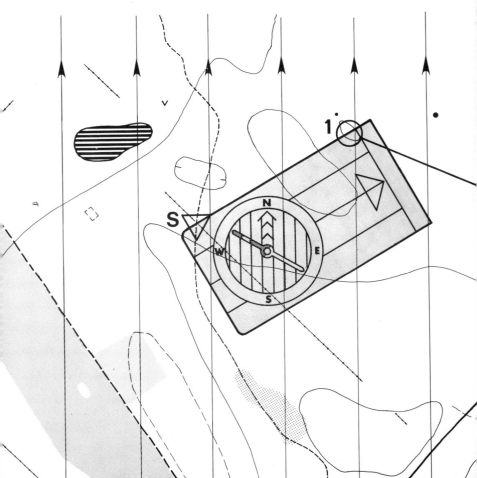

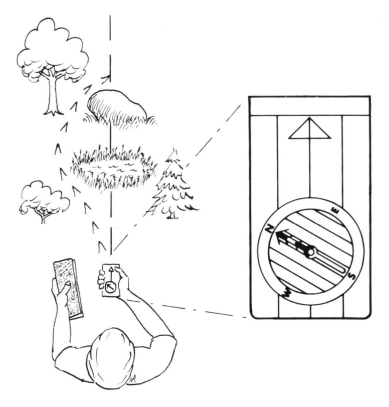

**Taking the bearing.**

*Step 3.* Finding your bearing. Remove the compass from the map and hold it level in your hand in front of your stomach. The *direction-of-travel* arrow must point away from you. Now turn yourself around until the North-indicator (red) end of the needle is pointing in the same direction as the *North* arrow in the compass housing. **Watch out:** Be sure that both the red end of the needle and the *North* arrow point in the same direction.

The *direction-of-travel* arrow now points towards your destination. If you want to know the bearing in degrees, although you don't really need to for running at the bearing, you can read it on the dial on the rim of the compass housing above the *direction-of-travel-arrow* (the dials are usually graduated only every two degrees).

Now let's see what we actually did here. First, we located the line of direction to travel (in step 1). We then transferred to the compass the angle between the North lines of the map and the direction of travel (in step 2). In step 3 we transferred this angle to the terrain by making the *North arrow* point to North, thereby finding the bearing to the destination. Now you can just follow the *direction-of-travel arrow* to your destination.

*Running on Bearing.* Using your map and compass you have taken the bearing and are ready to move on to your destination. Here is how you proceed:

*Step 1.* Holding the compass level in front of your stomach as mentioned previously, double check to be sure that the *magnetic needle* still covers the *North arrow* and that both of them still point North in relation to the map.

*Step 2.* Next you want to take your sighting. To do this, you look down at the compass, sight along the *direction-of-travel arrow* and then look up maintaining the direction of the sighting. Pick a landmark some 100 to 200 feet ahead of you in this direction. (Distance is hard to estimate at first—maybe it'll help to remember that the distance between home plate and first base is 90 feet and that a football field is 300 feet.) The landmark can be a tree, a patch of grass or something else easily recognizable. You don't have to use the compass again until you have reached that spot.

*Step 3.* Take the easiest route to the object avoiding bushes and other hindrances. You will continue in the correct direction as long as you keep your eye on your landmark.

*Step 4.* At the landmark you repeat the sighting procedure again and so on until you reach your destination. Shorter distances between the sighting places will give the most accurate result because many small errors have a tendency to cancel out each other unless you make a consistent error.

Getting her bearing with
map and compass.

*Setting the Map.* Some people find working with maps pretty confusing at first. One thing for sure—it's a darned sight easier if the map is lined up with the way you will be going. To do this, you do what we call "setting," or orienting, the map—turning the map so that its features line up with the actual features of the terrain. This ensures, for example, that when you take a sighting from your present map location towards a hill shown on the map, you will find the actual hill in that very direction. It's done this way:

Step 1.  Place the compass on the map in front of you with the compass needle (pointing in any direction) close to a North line on the map.

Step 2.  Ignore both the North/South lines of the compass housing and the base plate and concentrate on the *magnetic needle.* Turn both the compass and map together until the needle is parallel to the *North lines* and the North end of the needle points towards the North edge of the map.

*Step.* 3 Remove the compass without turning the map—and the map is oriented.

Everything on the map should now line up with the terrain. If the map shows a building to the right side of the trail you are walking along, you should see the actual building if you look to the right. With the map set in this way, you can also work backwards to figure out your approximate location when/if in doubt. You can almost always spot a recognizable terrain feature to give you all the clue you need.

An orienteer always keeps his map oriented to make the navigation as easy for him as possible. For instance, he will hold the map upside down when moving in a southerly direction, and on its side when moving toward the East or West.

To practice map setting all you need is a map of the area and a clear outlook. Once up on the outlook it's great fun to orient the map and then try to find on the map the various features you see from your perch.

*Determining Position.* Although it is rarely needed in an orienteering meet, *determining position* (finding an unknown position) is a handy map and compass skill. For with this technique and your compass you can find your own position on a map very accurately, as long as you can identify a couple of visible terrain features on the map. This is, of course, an invaluable tool should you become lost in the woods and is also an aid in pinpointing a favorite fishing, or other activity, spot on your map. Basically, it involves finding the bearing to a feature and then plotting the bearing on the map, as follows:

*Step 1.* Aim *the compass towards the feature* as accurately as possible (let the compass rest against something for the best result).

*Step 2.* Without moving the compass, *turn the compass housing* until its *North/South Lines* are parallel with the *magnetic needle* and they both point in the same direction.

*Step* 3.   Put the compass on the map. Place one edge of the base plate over and pointing at the feature you aimed at. Maintaining this, *rotate the entire compass around the feature* until the *North/ South lines* in the compass housing (just the North/South lines, don't worry about the needle) become parallel to the map's North lines. In addition, the *North/South lines must point towards* the North of the map.

You are located on the map some place along the edge line of the compass. If you know what feature you are standing along (like a trail, stream, etc.), then your location is where the compass edge crosses your feature.

*Step* 4.   If you don't know where you are at all—having no good natural feature to pinpoint yourself by—you will need a compass bearing on *at least two* identifiable objects. Then, using a pen or a pencil, plot the bearing to each on the map. Where their paths cross will be your location.

As we have said, these techniques are seldom used during an orienteering meet, but can be very valuable knowledge when hiking or sporting in back-country areas. Just for fun do some practicing from a place with good views to see how close you can come to your actual location. One day you may be mighty glad you did.

OTHER COMPASSES

There are a number of other compass types available besides the protractor type described above. They all have their uses, but are not always good for orienteering. A common requirement for all of them is that the needle should be liquid dampened—the compass housing filled with a clear oil. (The shivering of the needles found in compasses not having this feature will prove quite disturbing when you hold the compass in your hand.) Here are some additional compass types. You'll find them illustrated in the compass collection photo.

**Plain Watch.**   This type resembles a rather ordinary stop watch. It enables you to travel safely in a general direction but with only low accuracy.

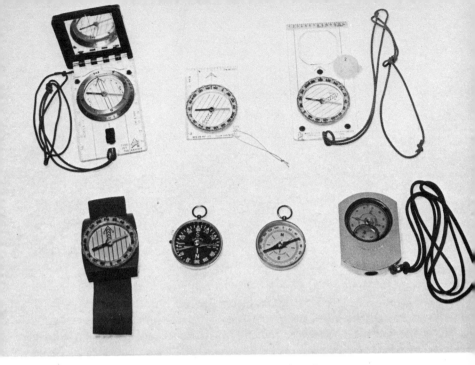

*Compass collection. Top row* (left to right): (1) Silva Ranger compass, a mirror compass; (2) basic orienteering compass; (3) competition orienteering compass (with pace counter and detachable scale). *Bottom row* (left to right): (1) wrist compass; (2) watch compass (with luminous dial); (3) plain watch compass; (4) Prismatic compass by Suunto.

**Wrist.** Resembles the plain watch type but has a wrist band. It is often preferred by ski-orienteers and ski-tourers as it leaves your hands free and also meets the main navigational problem—a fairly simple one—to judge if a trail heads out (goes) in the direction you want or not.

**Lensatic (Army) or Prismatic.** These offer excellent sighting devices but cannot be used directly on a map to take a bearing. This has to be done with a separate protractor. Suunto has an especially nice design which works very well in mapping because of its very high accuracy.

**Mirror.** This type has both a protractor and a sighting device. It can be used directly on a map and is very useful for either setting courses or mapping. This type is also the best for high-country trips. A *handy extra:* the mirror serves also as a good personal mirror.

## COMPASS DECLINATION

Declination (the fact that in most places magnetic North and true North differ) is something that an orienteer should never have to worry about in the field. All specially prepared orienteering maps are drawn with North lines toward *magnetic* North. And— any other map to be used should have magnetic North lines drawn on the map before it is used.

In case you do have to compensate for declination and you don't have a compass with permanent compensation adjustment (there are such compasses), here's how:

1. The angle (declination) between true and magnetic North should be stated on the map somewhere, normally in the margin. (Note: the declination will change with time, but less than a degree over a ten-year period. Most other information on a map is then also completely outdated and the map should be replaced anyhow.)

2. If the declination is West, add the declination to your reading before you head out. It might make it easier for you to remember that you must add if you memorize this line: "*Declination West, compass best.*"

3. If the declination is East, subtract the declination from your reading. To this goes the following memory backup: "*Declination East, compass least.*"

In the case when you work the other way—transferring a sighting to the map—you also must compensate according to the rules above, but with the procedure reversed. And be sure to do the compensation before you lay the compass on the map.


## WORDS OF CAUTION

A compass nearly always points in the correct direction even if you sometimes feel it should read something else—so, follow the compass. However, magnetic irregularities can be found in areas with iron ore deposits, so stay on the alert for such places. Also, always use the compass well away from any iron or nickel objects like metal ski poles, water pumps and power line towers. Once

Using the *determining position* technique described earlier (on page 63), this hunter can leave his favorite hunting area secure in the knowledge that he can find his way back another day.

when out mapping, one of your authors encountered strange readings in a certain spot. An abandoned well nearby was the culprit: all it took was one projecting metal pipe. It was necessary to move some 30 feet away before the compass could be trusted again.

Also, some words of caution are appropriate about storing your compass. It is alright to store it together with other compasses or near iron parts. But you must keep a compass away from anything that can generate changing magnetic fields like electric equipment or the ignition system of a car.

A *case in point:* one of us got a real surprise one year at the starting line of the Canadian championship. We had received the maps, and had taken the bearing towards the first control. Imagine the surprise—when turning to line up the North arrow and needle—to find oneself facing the opposite direction from all the other starters. Indeed, quite odd. On checking with the other runners sure enough—the needle was reversed! The race was finished only by remembering that the white part, instead of the red, now pointed North. As it happened, the compass had laid in the glove compartment of a car for a while and had become reverse-magnetized from the magnetic pulses from the ignition coil. A lesson for us all.

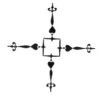

# Personal Equipment

**B**EFORE WE GO ON to the techniques of orienteering, let's look for a moment at the other equipment—besides a map and compass—that you will need to tackle an orienteering course. Bear in mind that the emphasis of the sport is participation and having fun, not fashionable trappings. A do-your-own-thing approach is just fine, as long as you are comfortable and protected. Since orienteering is enjoyed under widely varying conditions—from Nova Scotian dampness and cold, to California's or Georgia's sun and heat—use your own discretion as to what would be suited best to your area and weather conditions. *Above all . . . be comfortable!*

## Footwear

Orienteers probably display a wider variety of shoes than any other group of athletes. At orienteering meets you will see almost everything on feet from heavy hiking boots to light track shoes. At one orienteering clinic, although we certainly don't recommend it, a girl orienteer even came barefoot. The reason for this variety, besides personal preference, is the wide range of terrain found with the sport.

The purpose of the shoe, besides keeping your feet protected, is to give support to the foot–ankle area and to provide some

"Knobbies"—their waterproof tops and studded soles work especially well.

traction at the same time. Remember, orienteering courses traverse all types of terrain: slippery slopes, boulder fields, muddy logging roads, brambles and sometimes wetlands. Some examples of footwear used in orienteering are described here (note, too, the footwear photo).

*Hiking Boots.* Boots are warm, dry and provide lots of support. They are good for the beginner who isn't in much of a hurry. However, hiking boots are heavy: remember the old hiker's adage, "an extra pound on the foot equals five pounds on your back." Nonetheless, since orienteering is often a game of the "tortoise and the hare," it makes sense for those who travel slowly and steadily to use good solid boots—they beat the runners many times.

*Track Shoes.* This type of shoe is quite popular among the entries we see, probably because they are quite versatile. Besides for orienteering, they can be used to train, jog, play tennis or whatever. Groups that generally jog and walk the courses favor them and for these purposes they are fine, light and supportive.

Several track shoe companies are now making models with nylon uppers and fairly thick soles which seem almost ideal for orienteering purposes. It is inevitable that the shoes will get muddy and wet while orienteering; the nylon shoes can then be thrown in the washer, laces and all. If you're in the market for a pair of shoes, look for models with good support at the heel and arch and which have thick soles that will give you some cushion and traction.

*Tennis Shoes.* Tennis shoes are not highly recommended, but can be used in the pinch. Why? Because they are made for a game played on a smooth, level surface. Orienteering, on the other hand, is played on one of the roughest surfaces imaginable—the earth's natural face. If you are trying orienteering for the first time and don't have boots, you probably won't get injured wearing sneakers if you're not in too much of a hurry. But, if you plan to really get into the sport, get a pair of something that will protect your feet more than sneakers.

*Orienteering Shoes or "Knobbies."* These are the ultimate. Knobbies are similar to track shoes, but are made of waterproof reinforced nylon with studded soles. They are of foreign design and manufacture and have only recently been imported to America; consequently, they may be hard to find. Since they are made with orienteering specifically in mind, they conform best to the needs outlined above. If you plan on lots of serious orienteering, they are a good investment. (For names of suppliers in the United States, see appendix.)

*Other Shoes.* There are several other types of footwear which might suit your needs while orienteering. Soccer shoes appear to work satisfactorily in the woods; the studs are short and knobby, thus aiding in traction. Field hockey shoes look like they would do well too, and although we haven't seen them in action, the multi-studded football shoes that pros wear while playing on artificial turf might also be a possibility.

### SOCKS

Just a word about what is under the shoe. Socks are necessary; the thickness and number determined by the fit of your shoes or boots. They should be comfortable—loose but not lumpy. But a word of caution: if you want your wife, girlfriend, or whoever does the laundry in your house to become an orienteering fan, don't wear those new white sock of yours. Socks somehow often manage to get destroyed in the excitement of orienteering. For the sake of family tranquility, use an old pair of colored socks.

Having warned you against nice new white socks, we should add that white socks are indeed good for beginners until their feet are toughened. White is much safer next to freshly broken blisters.

## Clothing

No matter how you decide to take on an orienteering course, it's going to be a fairly strenuous undertaking. If you have done much hiking or jogging, you know that they generate a good deal of body heat. Because of this, orienteers dress much like hikers, and the faster ones dress like runners. Loose fitting, comfortable clothes are best. Let common sense be your guide and don't worry what you look like. Orienteering courses are going to take you off the beaten path and sometimes through some rather thick brush, so be sure you are well protected. There will be few spectators to laugh at your dress.

### TOPS

In keeping with the season, a T-shirt or sweat shirt will do. Leave your good sweaters at home—they would only risk being ripped. Your pace of travel will determine the number of layers you require. You can always take off a sweat shirt or windbreaker

***Suited up.*** Although certainly not necessary, specially designed orienteer-ing suits work well in the field. Offering welcome protection in rough terrain, the material is light, breathable and rip-resistant; the chest pocket proves very handy for accessories.

and tie it around your waist, but once you're in the woods you can't add a layer you don't have with you.

## BOTTOMS

There are a number of options here—your choice being dictated mainly by temperature and the voracity of the local undergrowth. Few orienteers wear shorts, and those few who do also don special protective knee socks to help fend off the briars. But, a warning: check with the meet organizer before you take to the woods in shorts.

In the long pants department, almost anything can be worn that will protect your legs. Sweat pants are commonly worn. Dungarees seem to do alright, as long as they don't fit too snugly. But think twice before you wear that new stretchy nylon warm-up suit for anything but warming up; they snag too easily.

## ORIENTEERING SUITS

Like orienteering maps and orienteering boots, orienteering suits are designed expressly for the needs of the sport. They are not required; in fact, few of them are seen aside from at the national championship meets. The suits consist of two parts: top and bottom, both made of light, breatheable, rip-stop nylon. The shirts are long-sleeved and have a front pocket for accessories. The pants are fairly loose and made along the lines of sweat pants. The suits have a decided advantage in hot weather and during two-day meets. At the end of the first day, they can be washed and hung on the line —drying time is remarkably short. It's not much fun starting an orienteering course in soggy dungarees.

## HEAD GEAR

To some, head gear may seem strictly optional equipment, but there are many times, especially in extreme temperature ranges that a hat or some kind of head protection is very helpful. In warm weather, it can be a real chore to read a map with beads of sweat streaming down your face. A good solution to this problem can be borrowed from golfers. Golf visors are light and shade the eyes at the same time. Others prefer head bands, baseball caps or nothing at all. It's up to you.

In the fall or early spring, mornings can be nippy, necessitating warmer head gear. Stocking caps or ear bands are the most popular, especially before and after a race.

# Accessories

## MAP CASE

As mentioned before in the map section of the *Map and Compass* chapter, map cases are most helpful. They keep the map fairly clean, dry, and supple, allowing you to fold the map in various dimensions. Map cases can be found at some sporting goods and stationery stores; the heavy-duty plastic envelopes available through business-supply houses also work nicely. Medium-thick poly (4 mil or 0.1 mm) is a good material to work with.

*Map case in operation.* Note that the clear plastic allows a good view of the map below the compass—at the same time keeping the map free of any dampness in the grass or ground. It offers the same protection against rain.

Map cases are also good receptacles for your score card and course-description sheet. Just remember to tape up the end of the case once extra items are inside. These critical bits of paper always seem to want to escape just when you need them most.

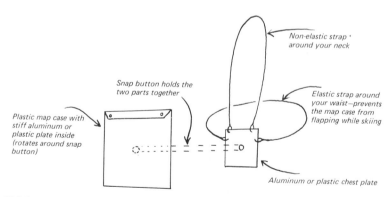

Non-elastic strap around your neck

Snap button holds the two parts together

Elastic strap around your waist—prevents the map case from flapping while skiing

Plastic map case with stiff aluminum or plastic plate inside (rotates around snap button)

Aluminum or plastic chest plate

*Ski-O map case.* The design of this do-it-yourself ski-O map case allows easy use on skiis. The center snap-button permits the orienteer to rotate the map in the direction of travel as he reads it, while the straps hold the case, freeing the skier's hands. For compass, a wrist compass suffices.

## FOOD

If you are not the highly competitive type, you might want some type of sustenance along your way; though even the fastest orienteers have been known to stop at especially attractive berry patches. At a meet in early August in New Hampshire, in the midst of a very long course, all the Blue-course competitors stopped frequently to sample the delicious blackberries along the route.

If it's the wrong time of year for berries, you might consider putting some dextrose or sugar cubes in your pocket before you start. Almost any high-carbohydrate, high-energy food will give you —and especially your mental processes—a lift as you orienteer. Be careful of chocolate bars, however—they quickly melt if stored close to your body, although you can find tropical, or non-melting chocolate bars, at some hiking stores.

We will reserve comment on the more elaborate menus that some picnickers bring along to meets, except to say that your imagination is the limit as long as it fits in a rucksack.

## WATER

If you are orienteering in a fairly uncivilized area, check with the meet promoter as to whether the running streams are drinkable. If so, there is nothing more refreshing than a cool drink of fresh water along the way. However, we wouldn't recommend you try this too near an urban area. In hot weather, a well organized meet should have water stops on the longer courses; but wayfarers might want to tote a well-filled canteen—to help keep the spirits high.

## INSECT REPELLENT

A good repellent is a must for late spring or summer orienteering in most parts of the United States and Canada. The most effective brand—at least it's our favorite—is "Woodsmen's Lotion," a combination of mostly pine tar and creosote. It keeps *everything* away—very often including even your fellow orienteers. Other first aid supplies should be available from the meet director if needed.

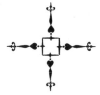

# Orienteering Techniques

O RIENTEERING IS indeed a multifaceted sport despite the fact that it only has two main ingredients—to travel around a course and to navigate the way. Of these two, the travel part —generally hiking or running—is quite straight forward. At least, it is compared to the art of navigation, which can be very complex and involves many different techniques. And it is at this point that we get into the many appealing aspects of the sport.

You don't have to be a super athlete to enjoy or to do well in the sport. Instead you can compensate for your body's lack of speed and power with clever navigation—and maybe end up at the top of the prize list, or at least get full satisfaction from knowing that you found every control "right on." Orienteering thus is a mental sport as well as a physical one—something that is quite unique. Indeed it is "cunning running," as a British slogan goes. It's often impossible to determine which is most important—the running or the cunning—that varies from course to course. But to be an elite orienteer you must master both, plus have the right type of psyche. A perfect race takes, for example, at least an hour of perfect concentration during hard physical work.

Fortunately few of the navigation skills are needed at a novice's first experience with the sport. A beginner's course should be designed so that just everyday common sense is needed to reach the finish line. However, as you move up to more advanced courses, more and more knowledge of specific techniques is required. These techniques are often learned from experience but you can spare yourself a lot of the frustration of missed controls by reading up on, and working with, these more advanced techniques before you enter the harder courses.

It is, however, impossible to master everything instantly so have patience. Typically it takes two to five years to become a top level (elite) orienteer. You just gradually do things faster and faster—with enough practice the different techniques become routine. For example, if you only need to consult the map 5 seconds every time fifty times on a course instead of 10 seconds one hundred times, you can cut at least 12½ minutes from your overall time without any extra workload.

*Learning the ropes.* Here a youngster is copying the day's course onto his own map. It isn't always easy at first.

## Common Techniques

The rest of this chapter describes a number of orienteering techniques that are commonly used. Also given are several useful hints designed to help you to cut corners. The techniques are given in the order in which you will experience the problems they deal with, rather than in order of importance. Most of the techniques can be individually mastered through the exercises described in the next chapter on training. (The following list sorts out these techniques by skill level; beginners should concentrate on the B's, working up to the M's as they become more advanced.)

TECHNIQUES AND THEIR
LEVEL CLASSIFICATION

*B=Basic*      *M=More advanced*

| | | | | |
|---|---|---|---|---|
| B | Course Plotting | | M | Traffic Light |
| B | Thumbing | | M | Green Route Selection |
| B | Control Card and | | B | Map Skimming |
| | Definitions | | B | Collecting Features |
| B | Reading the Map | | B | Handrails |
| M | Distance Judging | | M | Rough Map Reading |
| B | Route Choice | | M | Check Off Points |
| B | Control Extension | | M | Contouring |
| B | Aiming Off | | M | Climb/Distance Relations |
| B | Attack Point | | M | Ground Cover/Distance |
| M | High Approach | | | Relations |
| B | Precision Compass | | B | Mapping Problems |
| M | Precision Map Reading | | B | Misses |
| B | Control Finding | | M | Night Orienteering |

COURSE PLOTTING

At most beginner and local meets, the participants must copy the course from a master map over to their own individual maps. It is of the greatest importance that you do this copying absolutely correctly. If you have mismarked a control the chances are very slim that you will just run across it—unless you come upon a friendly soul running the same course who is nice enough to help you out. Most experienced orienteers work pretty much in this fashion:

1. Begin with the start, pinpointing it carefully (you might want to label this S or Start); then copy the controls in order.

2. Identify on the master map the feature of the first control point to be copied off and the nearest shown feature, as well as the direction and relative distance to that feature.

3. Then find some other eye-catching main features close to the control point. Try to "photograph" the distances and directions from these main features to the object.

4. Moving over to your map, locate the eye-catchers. Then spot the control object at about the distances and directions from these eye-catchers you feel correct.

5. Verify that the object relates to the nearest features as it should. *If something doesn't feel correct, do it over again.*

6. When you are sure, draw a circle of about ¼-inch (or 6 mm.) diameter around the point, and with the point in dead center. Then write down the control number near the control but try to avoid obscuring any important details.

7. Using the same technique, copy off the next control, write in the control number and then join this control and the previous one with a line. The numbers and joining lines will help to prevent you from taking the controls in the wrong order.

Be sure to do all your plotting with a waterproof pen.

Remember: you can use the beginner course on the fold-out map for a few trial runs.

Some at-home practicing of course plotting should probably cut down the time you will need for this chore to less than a quarter of the time used for your first try. But don't spend too much time perfecting this technique because most big meets nowadays issue premarked maps—a welcome service.

### THUMBING YOUR WAY

Once your map is copied, you must protect it in some way while you are out on the course. Otherwise it might get quite illegible just from wear—not to mention what happens if it rains. The best way to carry the map is to fold it inside a clear plastic pocket of medium-thick poly (see map case section in *Personal Equipment* chapter). The thick plastic prevents permanent creases from forming regardless of how the map/map case is folded.

This flexible map case also enables you to use the popular and time-saving technique called "thumbing." This is the technique of folding and holding the map so you can use your thumb as a continual pointer to your then current location. *As you move over the land, your thumb moves (with you) over the map.* In this way, every time you look at the map you can fast-focus on your current position instead of having to search over the entire map area. Thumbing not only saves time during a race but also eliminates most chances of parallel errors, *i.e.*, mixing up two adjacent (or nearly so) areas with basically the same main features.

With this technique and some practice you should be able to become quite proficient at running and map reading simultaneously. This, of course, saves even more time.

*The "thumbing" technique.* With the map well protected in its case, the thumb carefully, and easily, follows the orienteer's precise path as he moves along. With this technique "running" the course is smoother and less error-prone.

## CONTROL CARD AND DEFINITIONS

The control card and the definition (or control clue/code) slip are two other things that you have to carry along on your way around. But where?—they always need to be easily accessible.

One method preferred by many is to have them stored right in the map case—back to back with the map. You can prevent them from slipping by fastening with pieces of tape or a staple. You don't need to take the card out at the controls—just punch right through the soft map case. (You may have to replace your map case more frequently using this technique—eventually the case will get pretty "punchy" and no longer be very waterproof—but it is a convenient and time-saving technique.)

Another way is to keep the card and the slip in a small but strong zip-lock plastic pouch fastened with a safety pin to the front of your shirt. Again the card may be punched through the plastic. A slight advantage here is that with care you don't have to lose your thumb-pointer grip on your map while punching. Some runners prefer to have their clue sheet in a similar plastic bag taped to a shirt sleeve.

Whatever method you prefer to carry your definition slip, *the important thing is that you use it.* When you come to a flag, check that the control codes match. At the same time check the code, as well as your map, to find out where the next control is located so you don't make mistakes like searching for a marker at the foot of a cliff when it sits up top. Your clues will tell you all this.

## READING THE MAP

You should always keep your map oriented while you navigate between the controls, *i.e.,* hold the map so its North is always directed towards *magnetic* North. Directions on the map and on the ground will now match. For example if the map shows a knoll West of your location while traveling South, you will see that particular knoll if you look to the right—which should be West. This also means that you hold the map upside down if you go South and sideways while heading East or West. Naturally, for any direction you fold the map so you can use your thumb-pointer grip, once you've got it perfected.

*Don't cheat on this.*

With the map oriented so features on the map and on the terrain match and fall in place together, it is much easier to interpret what you see and to orienteer by just reading the map.

To start with you must consult the map frequently, but after some practice you should be able to memorize almost automatically what features you should expect to see next. You will also learn to project a mental image of what type of terrain you will run into. Will it be easy or difficult running? Vague or obvious map reading? You will often base your decisions as to what route to take to a control on this projected mental image of the terrain. But this takes time. Experience is your prime teacher in learning to master creative map reading.

## DISTANCE JUDGING

Knowing all the time where you are is the hallmark of a good orienteer. A good help in this is to be able to determine accurately how far you have gone away from the previous place located. This means being able to measure distances on the ground as well as on the map.

*Pace Counting.* Pace counting is an old method of measuring distances, but a good and simple one, so that is what today's orienteer uses. We, as well as the Roman soldiers, count double steps, *i.e.*, a count every time we put down the right foot (or left). By the way, the old definition of a mile—the distance that the average Roman soldier covered with 1,000 double steps—still holds true amazingly well. Try it some time. You might overshoot a bit because we are quite a bit taller nowadays compared to the Romans, but still . . . .

ONE WAY. For measuring the distance on the map, a couple of different methods can be used. One is to work in hundreds of meters and use a compass with a clicker-counter to record the number of hundred meters you have covered (see the compass collection photo in the *Map & Compass* chapter for a clear picture of this type counter). The measuring can be done with the millimeter scale on the compass—knowing how many millimeters equals a hundred meters (or compare the measurement against the map's scale). Or you can get the reading directly by using a compass with a scale (interchangeable or drawn on a piece of tape) graduated in hundreds of meters for the particular scale of the map in use. (See the next page for several handy scale samples.)

Now you have to pace count the number of hundreds of meters that you measured. But first you must know how many paces you must take for each hundred meters; and preferably this also for different speeds and terrain. Here are some typical values: hiking (60), running in dense woods or up hill (45), running on flat, wooded ground (40), running on a trail or down a moderate downhill in woods (35). *Each time you come to a count that equals a hundred meters in the type of terrain you just went through, you click the counter.*

When the clicker reads the same as the measured number of hundred meters you should have less than a hundred meters (or a little over 300 feet) left to go to the destination point. Continue an appropriate number of steps to adjust for the fraction that the measured distance overshot the whole number of hundred meters you figured. You should now be right at the point!

If you don't have a counter on your compass, you must instead keep a running tally of the number of hundred meters you have covered each time a hundred-meter count ends. Perhaps counting on your fingers by holding all fingers bent at the start and then opening up one for each hundred meters would be an easier way for you.

A SECOND WAY. A second technique to measure distances on the map is to figure entirely in paces. But first, in advance, you must develop a measuring scale calibrated in your average steps (*in 10's*) for the particular scale of the map that you are going to use. Tape that scale to your compass. You simply read on this scale the number of steps you should count to reach a certain point; and then just start running and counting. You can compensate for different terrain runabilities by adding or skipping over five or ten counts every time your counting reaches a multiple of hundred. *Many consider this the simpler way as it doesn't involve keeping*

## SAMPLES OF SCALES FOR MEASURING DISTANCES:

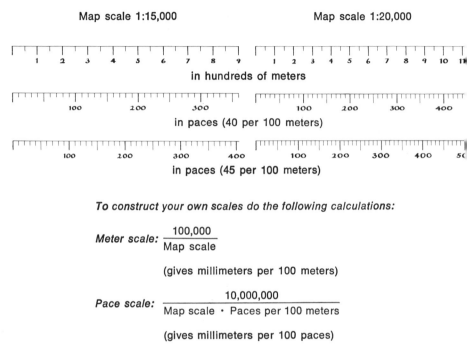

Map scale 1:15,000          Map scale 1:20,000

**in hundreds of meters**

**in paces (40 per 100 meters)**

**in paces (45 per 100 meters)**

*To construct your own scales do the following calculations:*

*Meter scale:* $\dfrac{100{,}000}{\text{Map scale}}$

(gives millimeters per 100 meters)

*Pace scale:* $\dfrac{10{,}000{,}000}{\text{Map scale} \cdot \text{Paces per 100 meters}}$

(gives millimeters per 100 paces)

*Distance judging aids.* The orienteer can use these sample scales and formulas, combined with some preliminary figuring and pace counting, to work up a handy auxiliary guide against which to measure his progress in the field—the guide to be taped on his compass.

track of the meters—and well worth the advance preparations.

It's a good idea for a serious competitor to develop the habit of pace counting. It can save you many valuable seconds over the years. However, you only measure the distance against the map beforehand when you are aiming for an important point, such as a control. The rest of the time you just keep the count in reserve as a back-up, doing the actual measuring steps on the map only if something goes wrong. Restart the counting every time you reach a point that you can identify positively. We'll be talking more about this as we go along.

ROUTE CHOICE

Route choice is the very heart of orienteering. This is what makes orienteering unique among running events. It allows a runner to select the route around a course that fits just him, his running style, his navigation skills, his psyche, and his experience. Actually route choice is a very complex subject and difficult to learn from theory only. Doing is the best learning method, giving you the experience and routine needed as a basis for good route decision. But some theorizing can be of good help at times, and what follows should help the beginner to at least understand the terms, and begin to realize what he'll find in the field.

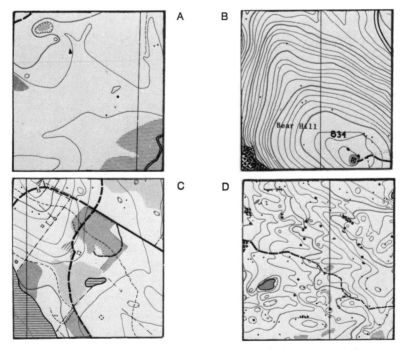

*Terrain rules supreme.* The wise choice of route and which techniques to use are governed by the terrain to be crossed. Here, A and B are basically the same type of area—both with little detail, but one flat and the other hilly. Each would require a different technique. Similarly, both C and D have considerable detail, but in area C many are man-made and easy to recognize. Here, too, each would suggest a different technique. The seemingly unrelated straight thin lines appearing on the spot maps throughout are the North/South lines from the full-scale original.

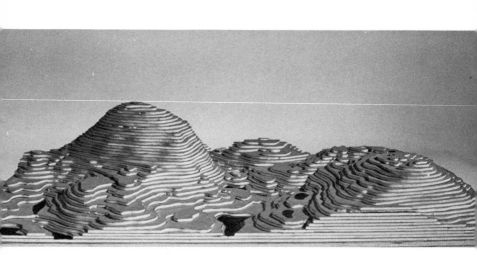

*Route choice.* An eye-level view gives additional perspective on the importance of terrain in wise *route choice.* To get to a control at the rear of the hill on the left, would one go over or around? How best would one reach a control on either side of the largish front-center water area from the other—without swimming or wading? Read on.

In competitive orienteering you try to complete the course in the shortest time possible. But you also want to place well every time—consistency is a top priority. To avoid misses you often have to use slower but safer routes. And this is, of course, even truer for the beginner. You always try to find an optional balance between desire for speed and need for avoiding mistakes. At the same time that you are making your route choice, you also commit yourself to the methods and techniques you will use between the controls. This interaction goes on all the time you are in the field. These techniques will vary from leg to leg of the course for one and the same runner, and depend very much—as does the route choice—on the type of terrain to be crossed.

Actually it is the terrain that rules what route to take and consequently what techniques to use. In the varying forms of the terrain the orienteering problems lay and wait for you. The course-setter can sharpen or vary these problems by his placement of the controls but it is the terrain that rules. It's an exciting challenge to solve and overcome these problems in a quick, and hopefully elegant, way and be able to find the flags "right on." Proper route choice selects the winner equally as much as the finding of the marker—although the latter is talked about much more.

## CONTROL EXTENSION

It's best to start to analyze a leg (section of the course between controls) by taking a look at the control you are headed for. What type of feature is it and where is it located? A control that is placed along a linear feature like a trail or stream is naturally much easier to find. Once you have reached the vicinity, you just follow along that feature until you see the flag. But many control features are physically quite small, e.g., knolls, boulders, etc. Nevertheless, the same technique as for the trail often can be used. Try to "extend" the control by checking to see if the control is located along or near a linear feature—the *boulder* might be at the edge of a particular piece of swamp on the map or the *knoll* directly on top of a definite ridge. Navigate to hit that linear feature as the prime target and then pick up the control when at the site.

*Control Extension.* In this example of *control extension,* A is extended to the left by means of the trail, which is easy to find. B's small boulder sits up on a ridge, which is used as its extension.

Control A: The clearing

Control B: The boulder

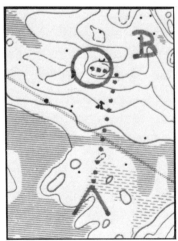

## AIMING OFF

When you are on a compass bearing towards a control that is located along a linear feature, you have a 50-50 chance to come out either to the right of the marker or to the left. If you don't see the flag right away, you don't know in what direction you should look for it. This dilemma will be avoided if you purposely aim your compass bearing to one side of the control. Then when you reach your extended control feature you are sure in what direction you should seek the marker.

**Control A: The stream junction**          **Control B: The boulder**

*Aiming Off.* A: When the stream is reached after *aiming off* to the left, it is followed back to the right where the marker should be visible in 100 to 150 meters. B is extended by the marsh and is very easy. Once the marsh is reached, it is a simple matter to follow along its edge to the left to the control.

## ATTACK POINT

After having determined what type of control feature you are headed for (*point* or *extended*) you should figure out the best way to reach that feature. Most times it is not possible to follow trails, streams, etc., all the way in to the marker. Instead you must reach the control or the extended control on a compass bearing taken from a point where you can locate yourself both positively and easily. *This last relocation place is called an attack point and must be easy to find, well defined, and as close to the control as possible.* Sometimes it is also possible to guide yourself in to the control from this point by careful map reading instead of by compass. Anyhow, we have now simplified the leg by inserting this straight forward check-off point just before the control.

If the major features on the bearing to a control are not well defined enough to serve as an attack point, you can often find a small, distinct point next to one. Use this smaller point as an attack point, but extend it with the big, easy-to-find feature.

Sometimes the control sits on such a big feature that no attack point is needed. The control or its extension fulfill the requirements of an attack point. This should be true most often for beginner courses.

Control A: The spur          Control B: The boulder

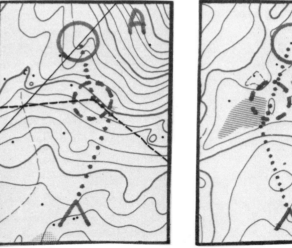

*Attack Point.* The trail before Control A fulfills all requirements for a good *attack point:* it cannot be missed and has a distinct point (the bend). Notice the *aiming off* for the bend. Control B is taken from the knoll (*attack point*), which is extended through the marsh.

## HIGH APPROACH

Something to keep in mind when you select an attack point for a control located on a slope is that the control is much easier to find if you come down on it from above. You face a much larger terrain section when you look down towards the valley bottom than when viewing a summit. Going down also makes it much easier to relate the map and the terrain.

Control A: The boulder

*High Approach.* The boulder is easier to see if approached from above instead of from a point below. The saddle (hump) serves as an *attack point.*

## PRECISION COMPASS

The final approach from the attack point in to the control feature is most often done using *precision compass*—and here might be a good place to turn back to the *taking a bearing* instructions in the "Compass" section of the *Map & Compass* chapter for a timely refresher session.

Precision compass is actually the only way to hit a control in areas with few details or where the map is unreliable. The more point-shaped the control location is, the more care you must put into taking the bearing and in sighting. Other situations where highest accuracy is required are when traversing slopes or in an area where recovering from a miss would cost a lot of time. Some helpful hints:

1. If the point is small or distant, stop completely every time you sight.

2. Keep your sighting landmark in view all the time to avoid mix-ups.

3. Pace count as accurately as possible during all precision compass work. Measure the distance before you leave the attack point.

These precautions will eat up some time, but will pay off in currency much valued by orienteers—consistency—by not missing *any* controls at *any* meets.

## PRECISION MAP-READING

At times, accurate navigation using the map only can bring you from the attack point to the control quickly and without encountering energy-consuming obstacles.

This *precision map-reading* is done by checking off every feature along the route while thumbing (keeping an accurate thumb-pointer). Remember to glance at the compass as you go to check that you maintain the correct direction. Also, as in precision compass work, measure the distance before you leave the attack point and then pace count.

Naturally precision map-reading can be done only in areas with lots of details. Also you must know that the map is of excellent quality: always avoid precision map-reading on the first leg with an unfamiliar map.

Control A: The cliff foot

*Precision Map-reading.* To reach Control A using *precision map-reading,* the pond (attack point) can be approached rapidly. There, map-reading in to the control begins—either going left of the pond and checking off: re-entrant, depression, re-entrant, right of marsh, across marsh, hill foot; or, going right and checking off: ridge, re-entrant, boulders, knoll/ marsh and hill foot.

CONTROL FINDING

After a meet, it is striking to notice how many people who didn't place well talk on and on about by how much they missed this or that control. Obviously a lot of minutes are lost near the controls. At least, that is the most apparent place to lose time. A bad route choice or a missed route is much harder to estimate time-wise.

What can you do to avoid these control misses? Here are some good rules to try to follow:

1. Always read the control description carefully. Look for the terrain feature, not the flag. Much time can be wasted if you look for a "top of the cliff" at the foot of the cliff—plus the energy to finally climb up there. Try to navigate yourself to the cliff top in the beginning. At the same time, memorize the control's code number to avoid punching a neighboring marker.

2. Extend the controls if possible (by making use of the natural terrain features). Make it easy for yourself. Don't use the same technique on all controls independent of size and location.

3. Slow down. Your brain works better under less strain. The slower pace gives you a chance to observe the surroundings better.

4. Concentrate. Keep everything under control—compass sightings, pace counts, features you pass, etc. It takes practice but you'll be surprised how quickly you learn if you concentrate. Ignore other runners.

5. Be extra careful with the first marker on a course. Experience shows that it is a critical one and easy to miss. It sometimes takes a while to get a good feeling for the map and terrain. Further, if not warmed up properly before starting, your body can be in slight shock after the sudden burst of activity. Psychologically it is very important to hit this first marker "right on." So, care really pays here.

*At the Control.* What you do at the control is also very important to your overall time. So—after you have located the flag, check the code before punching. Punch once—hard and in the proper box—an illegible punch can cause you to be disqualified. (Another time-saver: practice trying to maintain your thumb-pointer even while punching in.)

Move away from the control immediately while planning the next leg. But be sure to go in the correct direction—try to train yourself to remember this from the last look you had at the map.

*Punching in.* The idea is to be sure that the punch goes in the proper box on the control card. Here, one competitor is punching in right through her map case—this saves time.

## TRAFFIC LIGHT

Orienteering conditions and challenges, as we have said, are always changing—and can sometimes, as we shall see, be compared to a highway control system. For instance, with a big and easy attack point, you should be able to orienteer with emphasis on *speed* up to that point. But during the final distance in to the control, you had usually better use *safety-first* tactics—precision compass or precise map-reading, accurate pace counting, and reduced speed. Or, in other words, under this scheme of comparing your orienteering route to a highway system, your orienteering "light" shows a steady green, or occasionally flashing green, until you reach the attack point. There you receive a flashing red— proceed with greatest care.

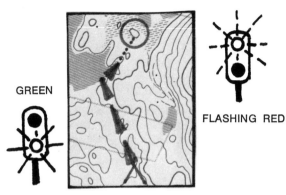

**GREEN**

**FLASHING RED**

Control A: The knoll

*Traffic Light.* It's "green light" and full speed ahead to the marsh. Once there, the marsh edge is followed to the right but with caution—*flashing green light.* From there, it's *flashing red light* from the tip of the marsh in to the marker—going slow to keep everything under control.

## GREEN ROUTE SELECTION

Having considered how best to approach and locate a control from an attack point, let's look at how best to approach that attack point quickly. Under *green route selection* you can use a rough type of orienteering from the previous control up to the attack point, trying to cover the distance as fast as possible. To minimize the time spent on map-reading, try to rely on map memory as much as possible and plan to navigate only between or along the major features of the map—roads, trails, streams, hills, swamps, etc. This way very few stops or slow-downs are needed for studying the map. Beyond this, a rough type of compass work is utilized to head you from one such big feature to the next.

Again, the type of features you base your route choice on is very much a matter of personal preference, strength and skill. As we have said, the type of terrain and vegetation that you envision ahead of you must be part of the decision making. It is a very complex matter, and experience is without doubt the best guide. Of the two extremes, one is the straight-line approach preferred by the *strong* runner who doesn't mind woods running and who also has mastered map-reading and compass running; the other involves long detours along roads and trails but which can take the *fast* runner just as quickly to the attack point. Thus, one man's *green route* might be another man's red—or yellow. Most of us usually work some place between these two extremes.

In the following sections we will deal with various techniques the orienteer can put to good use when he has a "green light."

## MAP SKIMMING

Orienteers like to see maps with a lot of details marked giving them an unlimited number of possible control check points. But in a meet, you only use these small features when precision orienteering into a control. Out on the first fast section of a leg, you don't have time to check off these details. You are only interested in the major features of the terrain. In fact, too many small details cluttering your mind might disturb your vision of the big features. Try to skim them away to make the major things easier to pick up, memorize, and use for your navigation.

## COLLECTING FEATURES

After having skimmed away the small details, your mental map should consist of a number of big, easy-to-find features. One of them should be your attack point (may be *extended*). Any of the remaining *collecting features* should be prominent enough for you to recognize even if you are running at maximum speed and strain. They should help orient you, even as you run long stretches quickly and use only fairly inaccurate navigation. A collecting feature should always be able to relocate you so you can concentrate on speed. Nonetheless, *always back yourself up with pace counting.*

The beginner will find that it takes time to learn to read a map this selectively and it's especially difficult when under pressure at a meet! Hilltop practice, as we said earlier, is a good training tool.

**Control A: The spring**

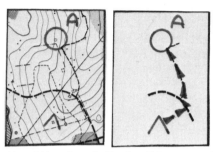

**Control B: The re-entrant**

*Map Skimming, Collecting Features and Handrails.* Even for a beginners' control like A it's useful to employ all three of these techniques. *Map skimming* makes it easier to detect the best route. The jeep trail makes a good *collecting feature* but aiming off should be used to insure finding the trail right away. The trail will then serve as a *handrail* leading to the sharp trail bend—the attack point for the control.

Control B is on a much more advanced leg. *Map skimming* makes it far easier to see that the best route is to run *rough compass* (see opposite) about 300 meters to the valley—the *collecting feature.* After a right turn, the foot of the slope serves as the *handrail* to the pass—the attack point. With these techniques the runner can concentrate on speed nearly all the way.

## HANDRAILS

Major features of the map left after skimming away the details can also be used as *handrails* to lead you ahead without the need to use the compass—much as a rope guideline leads one up a gang plank or a railing along a balcony. Naturally man-made objects like roads, trails, fields and fences are excellent handrails but topographical features can also work well for the advanced orienteer. Ridges or valleys can be utilized to guide you towards your attack point, as well as hydrographic features, e.g., streams, lakes or swamps. The idea behind handrails, as for collecting features, is to permit you to run at maximum speed with little time spent on map and compass. Learning to identify the good natural handrails takes time too, but it's worth it.

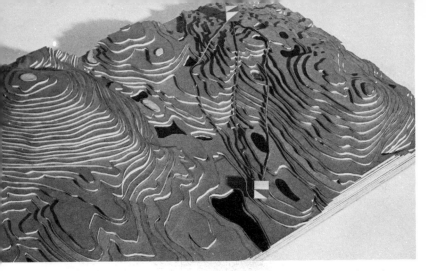

*Using handrails.* In getting from the control in the foreground to the one at the hillier rear, how much easier to move quickly along the natural depression (*handrail*) between elevations (center line) and then zero in more deliberately from there than to climb and figure all the way as one would taking either the left or right course.

### ROUGH COMPASS

In the *rough compass* technique the compass is most often used just to guide you quickly to a collecting or handrail feature. Normally you take the compass bearing according to the regular three-step scheme we learned in the *Map & Compass* chapter, but put less emphasis on accuracy in the sighting. Often you sight while running, holding the compass level some seconds to allow it to stabilize before taking a reading. You can run where the footing is easier even if it brings you off-bearing a bit, but try to compensate later, and *watch out* that you don't yield in one direction only. Naturally you verify the distance by your pace-counting techniques as you go.

If the feature you are aiming for is big, you just set the compass directly on a bearing that you judge to be correct. Or, still simpler: look only at the compass needle and keep an approximately correct angle between it and your course. On sunny days, you can take one sighting with your compass, register the position of the sun or its shadows and then run, maintaining that position.

### ROUGH MAP-READING

During *rough map-reading* you navigate your way through the terrain by following handrails and collecting features. To permit this, the area must be rich in big details. Naturally you use the thumb-pointing technique and back it up with pace counting. A well-trained map memory will save quite a bit of time. The skimmed map features should be large enough to permit you to consult the map while running.

## CHECK-OFF POINTS

This is a good tactic, where possible, for the ardent competitor. It allows a chance for a lot of speed—as long as one doesn't go astray. *Check-off points* are smaller natural features and can be of two types. One kind is memorized before you start out for use as you go—perhaps along a handrail to aid you in judging distances or as to when to change handrails. For example, running along a trail you might be looking for the second spur (protruding ridge) on the right (distance approximately 150 meters). There you plan to pick up a draw (gully) going to the left. Readily recalled check-off points can help you spot these vital features easily and quickly. Pick the type features for your check-off points that are easiest for you to work with. Experience will soon teach you which those are.

The other type of check-off point is memorized as you pass it—by making a mental note of at what distance the feature was seen. On passing the more obvious of these features you might want to restart your pace count. This mental list of features and their location can be of great help in retracing your route quickly in case of a miss.

*Contouring.* Without going too far afield, try to follow the same natural contour line as long as possible when moving from one control to another—using the map to help pick the best spot to do any necessary climbing. The example at *left* was fairly simple; the one at *right* took more thought and could perhaps have put contouring to even better use.

## CONTOURING

In hilly areas, maintaining the same elevation along the side of a slope—on the way to another feature—can save a lot of energy and time by avoiding climbs. Try to run on the contour. If you encounter ravines or gullies along the route, pick out a landmark on the other side of the obstacle and restart your contouring after reaching that landmark.

## CLIMB/DISTANCE RELATION

On most legs the course setter tries to discourage a "straight on" approach by placing the controls so that a major obstacle falls on the bee line. One such common feature is a hill, ridge, or a valley. But how much does a detour cost as opposed to doing the climb-

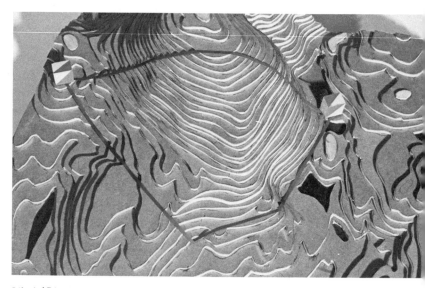

*Climb/Distance.* To go over or around? The two proposed routes between the control at left and the control at right shown here treat this orienteering problem head on. The condition of both terrain and runner are the chief factors and each case differs, but a good general formula is that 10 meters of climb equals 100 of flat distance.

ing? That obviously depends a lot on personal preference and fitness, as well as on the terrain runability. Assuming equal terrain, a rule of thumb is that 10 meters of climb equals 100 meters of distance. These 10 meters compare to three contour lines crossed on a map with 10-foot (3 m.) contour intervals, or two lines on a 5 m.-interval map.

## GROUND COVER/DISTANCE RELATION

Beside taking the topography into account, an orienteer should consider his running speed through different types of terrain and ground cover. How do long detours along trails pay off compared to going straight through the woods? Here again it's very much a matter of personal preference and strength. The former track runner zips along the trails, but the rugged woodsman gains by crashing right through the underbrush.

You can get some guidance from the figures below which are valid for an intermediate orienteer. The numbers are relative time units spent to cover the same distance in various environments. Training in woods-running will make the differences smaller than listed:

| Terrain | Time Unit |
| --- | --- |
| Road, good path | 1 |
| Open forest | 1½–3 |
| Forest with thick underbrush | 4–6 |

Woods with very uneven and rocky footing are as slow as the thick-underbrush forest. Even worse to cross than the above are the stream beds with their wet, slippery footing, criss-cross fallen trees, briars and tangles, etc. **A hint:** To avoid some of this treacherous footing, remember you can often follow such a stream by running parallel to it on higher and better ground.

## MAPPING PROBLEMS

Try to anticipate problems that you might have with your map. If an area is very flat and has few details, assume that the mapmaker had problems there. The features might be off a bit and are probably small. Keep your compass handy and the compass work accurate—and be sure to pace count.

*Changing Features.* Remember too that many features change with the season and weather conditions. Swamps, streams and ponds that are filled in the wet seasons might be completely dried out when there is a drought. So, a stream that you're counting on on your map may have completely disappeared when you reach it in the field. On the other hand, if it has been wet don't be surprised if you find a swamp looking like a pond. (When necessary consider the vegetation instead, i.e., a pond may look like a clearing and be grassy, and a swamp will still have its typical kind of bushes.)

And remember—a small stream bed is very hard to see on a dry fall day after the leaves cover it. So avoid using one as a collecting feature at the wrong time of year. Trails also change from season to season. They are easy to see in the spring, but when the vegetation is at its peak or after all the leaves are down, the smaller trails are very difficult to find. It is easy to run right over them without noticing. Just a few more reasons why the orienteer must stay alert at all times.

### MISSES

Sooner or later at some point while out on the course every orienteer will experience the eery feeling that something has gone wrong. You see a good-sized valley in front of you, but the route you're following on the map goes over a plateau. Strange! Or you are homing in on a control and your pace count runs out, but there is no marker in sight. Odd! *You missed.* And it won't work to say that the map-maker or the course-setter blew it—no, chances are you did!

*Getting Back on the Track.* Of course the best way to avoid having to correct misses is to stay on course (more about that in a paragraph or two) but, when the time does come for your miss— *what to do?*

RETHINK.  The best thing is: *Stop!* and *Think!* Don't just continue on or run around with the hope that you will see the marker. The odds are great you will only get more confused and lost. Try to retrace your route. What is your current pace count? Where were you last time you knew precisely where you were on the map? What check-off features have you passed since that? Did good running ground along the route somewhere divert you from your course for a longer stretch then intended? What good features can you see right now? After having gone through these questions, you should be able to figure out pretty well where you are. Maybe try to check out at least one of the features around you to verify your position and then just continue towards the control. But, *a word of warning:* it isn't always that easy.

If you can correct a miss this simply, you might be a future champion. Champions are said—besides being strong runners and excellent navigators—to be able to correct rapidly after a miss and then to orienteer directly on toward the control again. Most competitors don't have all the facts in hand necessary to do this this easily—probably because of slipping concentration, the latter often the reason for the miss in the first place.

RELOCATE.  If this mostly mental retracing doesn't give you any clue, you will have to find a feature that you can identify positively. Take a look around where you are standing now. If the immediate area is too indistinct or cluttered to help you relocate yourself, check your map and then run to the nearest major *collecting* or *handrail* feature. The sooner the better is the rule most of the time. Running around in circles normally just makes the miss bigger and bigger.

*Misses.* To either avoid or correct a miss, it's sometimes necessary to just stop, check the map and rethink a bit.

*Staying on the Track.*  As we just said, the best way to avoid having to correct misses is to stay on the track. Always know where you are and you will eliminate misses. That's not always an easy assignment if you are also trying to make good time, but the following routines will help:

1. *Modify* your navigation techniques according to the size of your destination.

2. Remember distinct features along your route and the distances to them.

3. Watch out for subtle course diversions sometimes followed because of especially good footing.

4. Watch out for parallel errors. Parallel error is one type of mistake that is sometimes very hard to recognize. In some areas, often the same type of features are found next to each other; e.g., ridges or valleys. It sometimes doesn't take much imagination to make one area fit another one, and you can spend an incredible amount of time looking for a control in the wrong area. Be very critical and carefully check the map again if something doesn't quite seem to fit. Or bail out to the nearest road.

5. Take it easy to the first control and remember to warm up.

6. Always pace count.

One Last Hint.    After having found that hard control at last, it's quite natural to say, "Now, I'm going to catch up," and then start out again at a high tempo. But chances are that tempo may be above your normal orienteering skill level and will only result in a new miss by a very discouraged orienteer. It's better to "cool it" a bit for a while.

## NIGHT ORIENTEERING

Although night orienteering is not too common yet in Canada and the United States, it is an interesting variation and deserves note. It also requires a considerable amount of orienteering skill— and some quite different techniques. We'll look at a few of these here.

As you can imagine, the narrow beam of light from your head lamp (you'll remember from the equipment chapter that we said you'd need a head lamp for night-O) will give you only a very limited field of view. This not only makes it difficult to locate your control, it also makes it very difficult to relocate yourself if lost. The advice, always know where you are, is especially important for a night orienteer.

A night orienteer finishes strong.

*Special Problems.* Many good daytime handrails are easy to slip by at night—even a power line is hard to see, as are the smaller trails. A 20-meter-high hill might as well be ten times its size—you will hardly notice the difference. Even big features like ponds and fields are hard to fathom. They are like looking into big black holes.

In fact, just reading the map can give you trouble. The difference between a blue and a black line is not so obvious at night and it's easy to misinterpret the map information or slip over details. And, of course, even your running time is reduced at night except along roads or major trails.

*Helpful Tips.* But, even though it is trickier than daytime orienteering, night-O is challenging and well worth the extra precautions. Here are a few hints.

1. Avoid shining your headlamp beam directly on your map or your night vision will be impaired for quite a while.

2. Hard rough orienteering and improvisation are bound to meet failure.

3. Be methodical.

4. Always pace count—as usual.

5. Extend and aim off at all features you try to hit.

6. Navigate more with the help of the bigger features which are more visible at night. Trails and roads are good and also allow fast running.

7. For extra safety, bring along a spare bulb, a small flashlight and maybe also a spare compass. Remember: *safety first is the rule* for all night-O.

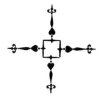

# Technique
# Training

Orienteering should be fun. Despite the various approaches to the sport, one common denominator among all orienteers is that they take part for their own enjoyment. It should follow that whatever one does to prepare for orienteering should also be enjoyable. Some become very involved, and will do whatever is required of them to improve their performances in competition, while others simply enjoy an occasional semi-programmed walk in the woods on the weekend, and couldn't care less about their results in terms of minutes and seconds. If they complete the course and meet all the challenges on the way, they are happy.

This chapter is aimed at the person somewhere between these two extremes: someone who enjoys orienteering, and has the urge to do at least a little better the next time out. If you are content with your style of orienteering, that's fine—there's no need to go any further in this chapter. Who's to say you're having less fun— or getting less out of the sport—than the experts on the Blue course? On the other hand, if you are striving to win the National Orienteering Championship or run the O-Ringen in Sweden, you probably will be disappointed in our training suggestions. Space does not permit all the sophisticated training exercises that do exist and which in Europe fill volumes by themselves. If you fall somewhere between these two extremes (which most of us do)— read on. But remember: whatever you do for training should enhance your enjoyment of orienteering and not create drudgery. *Orienteering is meant to be fun!*

Because so many skills go into a good orienteering performance, there is a wide variety of training available. Few other sports demand such a combination of physical and mental effort during a contest. The orienteer must constantly think on his/her feet: there are no huddles or time-outs in which to gather one's thoughts. From the word "go" until the finish. there must be constant thought while on the move. All the speed and endurance of a sub-four-minute miler will be for naught, if an orienteer's mind can't keep up with his legs. Because of orienteering's unique combination of physical and mental demands, orienteering training can be categorized in two basic areas:—*technique training* and *physical training*.

Practice spent in either of these areas will improve your orienteering. But like many other sports, the best practice is the game itself. The best way to get better at orienteering is to orienteer. It's that simple. But unfortunately, most of us don't have enough time to spend two to three hours every day charging through the woods. And adding to the problem, an orienteering course takes time and manpower to prepare. So, faced with the fact that orienteers cannot go to an orienteering meet daily, the training alternatives we suggest in this chapter are the next best thing.

## Technique Training

Participation in regular meets gives all-round training naturally, but to strengthen the effect of particular training techniques—to make them second nature, as it were—you need to run in a number of different special training exercises regularly. You'll find a good selection of these exercise-games to choose from here—games designed to train certain specific techniques. Naturally there are many variations that can be used. A differentiation has been made depending on how much organization is required and the exercises are split into two general categories:

1. *Informal group exercises* that do not require preorganization. These are best suited for small groups.

2. *Preorganized events* that have to be set up beforehand.

No doubt you and those you work out with will soon settle on your own favorites. However, do remember that many of the exercises can also be done *alone*, and without any prearrangements. Just pretend that the markers are in place and do the exercise just as you would with them there.

*Follow the Leader.* Training games can be fun as well as good exercise and good orienteering practice. Here, two budding competitors pursue the *follow the leader* exercise—with map.

A look at the accompanying chart will quickly pinpoint for you which games are designed to train which skills. The relative values of the different exercise-games are evaluated by points. A 1 denotes a game of intermediate training significance for a specific skill; a 2 indicates maximum training significance.

*Here are some informal group exercises . . .*

This group of games is best done with a small number of participants.

### FOLLOW THE LEADER

Unfamiliar terrain is a must for this exercise but it can be practiced in two ways:

1. *With a map.* All runners in a group of perhaps two to four have maps. Everybody should be aware of the starting point. One elected runner chooses a point some 1,000 meters away without telling the rest of the group where it is. It should be a not too difficult point. The leader orienteers (avoiding use of the compass) to the point; the rest of the pack follows, trying to find his route on their maps. Now and then he stops, at which point the rest should be able to tell him their position and how they got there. When the first point is reached, a new leader takes over. This is good practice in *map-reading* and *terrain-memorization* and is equivalent to route orienteering.

2. *Without a map.* Only the leader has a map. The chosen point must be very easy and the route short (100 to 150 meters), following handrail-type features. After the map man has reached the chosen point, the rest of the runners should try to point out what route they ran and where they are. This trains both *map and terrain memorization.*

### BERGVIK RUNS

This practice game, which got its name from the Swedish club that invented the game, is suitable for groups of two to four orien-

| | Terrain Memory | Map Reading | Map Memory | Distance Judging (Pacing) | Rough Compass | Precision Compass | Route Choice | Control Finding | Attack Point | Running | Course Setting |
|---|---|---|---|---|---|---|---|---|---|---|---|
| Follow the Leader | 2 | 2 | 2 | | | | | | | | |
| Bergvik Runs | | | | | | | 2 | | | | |
| Map-Memory Chase | | | 2 | | | | | | | | |
| Swapped Courses | | 1 | | 1 | 1 | | 1 | | | | 1 |
| Route Orienteering | | 2 | | 1 | | | | | | 1 | |
| Compass/Pacing Lines | | | | 2 | | 2 | | | | | |
| Line Orienteering | | 2 | 1 | | | | | | | | |
| Score Orienteering | | 1 | | | | | 1 | 1 | 1 | 1 | |
| Control Picking | | 1 | | | | | | 2 | 1 | | |
| Rough Orienteering | | | | | 2 | | 1 | | | 1 | |
| Assigned Routes Orienteering | | 1 | | | | | 2 | | | | |
| Blank-Map Orienteering | | | | 2 | | 2 | | | | | |
| Map-Memory Star Orienteering | | | 2 | | | | | | | 1 | |
| Control Plotting | | | 2 | | | | | | | 1 | |
| Mini-orienteering | | 1 | | | | | 1 | 1 | | | |
| Training Meets | | 2 | | 1 | 1 | | 2 | 1 | 1 | 1 | |
| Combi Runs | varies with the combination | | | | | | | | | | |

TRAINING GAMES & EXERCISES

teers of about equal ability. Together, they decide on a course of suitable length and difficulty with at least several controls. The runners start out on each leg at one-minute intervals (they might also assign different routes for each other before the start). As the controls are reached, the runners wait until all have reached the point; the first runner in can time the later arrivals. They then discuss the previous leg, plan the next leg and start out again in a new order.

Others may choose to re-join after a couple of controls. In this case, each runner should carry some small streamers along. When each runner arrives at a control, he/she hangs up one of his streamers unless he finds that all the other runners have already hung theirs in place ahead of him. In this case, he takes down all the streamers. At the pre-agreed waiting point, the runners check to be sure all the streamers have been picked up. If not, all go back to the disputed control to determine the correct point. After an analysis of the previous legs, the streamers are then redistributed and the runners head out again for a new set of controls. *Bergvik Runs* simulate very well a regular orienteering run and also give an immediate opportunity to *compare routes*. They also add some often welcome competitive spice to a group workout.

## MAP-MEMORY CHASE

This exercise is done in groups of two with runners of about equal skill. Runner A selects a point on the map which is easy to orient to and not more than a couple of hundred meters away. Runner B is allowed to study the leg for about a half a minute. He then tries to orienteer to the point just from memory. Runner A follows after with the map, checks the route and stops B if he is running away from the control. The runners rotate functions after each leg. This trains *map-memory* for B and *map-reading* for A.

## SWAPPED COURSES

This type training is normally done by two persons. From the common starting point each runner goes out and sets a short

(½-length) course of appropriate difficulty in a section of the area that is reserved for him. The participants return to the start area before a determined time. After some rest they swap courses and run the other person's course as a regular training-O. At the same time they pick up the streamers or flags that marked the controls.

This game simulates a regular training orienteering meet or a run on a course with permanent controls but also gives experience in setting courses. No timing is required.

Several persons may participate if the area is split so each person has an area. At the restart each runner goes out to all controls except his own. The markers have to be retrieved after all orienteers are back.

## And some preorganized events

This category of exercises is best suited for club training sessions or for training camps.

### ROUTE ORIENTEERING

This is a variation of orienteering that gives lots of practice in map-reading and distance judging. Route orienteering can be made suitable for all levels of orienteering proficiency by varying the route, but is especially good for beginners because the participants follow streamers all the way and could get lost only with great difficulty.

Use an area that is quite detailed. Put out streamers along a route that can be found on the map all the way by map-reading. Compass bearings should not be required. But—be aware that hanging out streamers is very time-consuming, as indeed is taking them down again, so don't plan a long course.

Place control markers at well-defined features along the route. Each participant should carry a pencil or pen, and at least one safety pin (more is safer), to use to mark the position of each control on his/her map; a small pinhole at the control point will do this without messing up the map. On the backside of the map he then circles the pinhole and writes the control number in the circle. At a beginner's event, there should be helpers stationed at each control to supervise.

At the finish, each runner's map is examined and the pinholes measured in millimeters (remember, a millimeter is only .0394 of an inch) against the correct location. For each full millimeter error, a time penalty is added to the final running time. This penalty might be 10 to 60 seconds per millimeter, depending on the difficulty of the course.

On advanced courses, pinpointing of objects away from the streamer route might be part of the exercise. In this case, the feature is best shown to the participants by use of a sighting device.

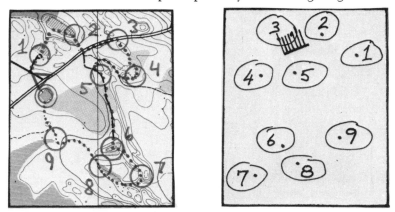

*Route Orienteering.* At left, an example of a *route orienteering* course, though for the purposes of this exercise no course is drawn on the participants' maps—streamers show the way. At right, the back side of a corrected map after the course is completed. All controls rate a perfect score except number 3 which is 4mm off.

COMPASS/PACING LINES

Here is an exercise that will help reinforce *compass skills*, but can also be used to correct *pacing* technique.

The organizer instructs the participants at the starting point to set their compasses to a certain degree reading—or better yet to take a bearing from a rough-sketch map with just the start and destination points shown. He should also indicate how far the runner should proceed at that bearing. In that direction, some 50 to 300 meters away, a line of streamers is set up perpendicular to the bearing. Numbered poster-board pieces are placed every 5 meters on the ground under the streamers. (Control cards are fine; but, if it's windy, whatever is used had better be weighted down.) At the correct point the sign should read 0. The boards to the left of the 0 sign are numbered −5, −10, etc., and to the right, +5, +10, etc. (A good rule of thumb is that in addition to the 0 number, you need at least one numbered-card location for each 10 meters of distance from the starting point to the streamer line.) It is important that the placement of the 0 sign be determined with highest possible accuracy using a sighting compass.

The participants are to read and record the number on the sign nearest them when they come to the line and then follow the streamers in one particular direction; e.g., to the right. At the end of the streamers, a new compass bearing is given and the exercise begins again. If the exercise is also used as a pacing check, the number of paces to the streamer lines should be recorded.

Afterwards, the participants can study the results to find out if

**Compass/Pacing Course.** Part of a suggested course for the *compass-pacing* training exercise. This exercise helps train taking bearings, as well as compass and pacing skills. A permanent *compass/pacing* practice course, if it can be arranged, is a great boon to orienteers—wayfarer and elite alike.

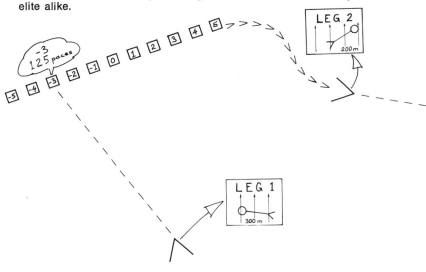

they are making consistent compass errors and/or how good their pacing is. The course can be run several times at different speeds to check the runners' accuracy further.

This exercise can be made competitive by adding time penalties based on how far off from the o point the runner was. But, in this case, the cards are numbered consecutively with only the organizer knowing the o point. The value of this exercise can be further increased by arranging it so that the different legs are run through different terrain types—open woods, dense bush, uphill, downhill, along a hillside, etc.

## LINE ORIENTEERING

The route that the runners have to follow is shown as a line on the master map (everyone should be sure to copy the course very carefully). Along this route are placed unmarked, easily visible controls. The participants start out in 1- to 3-minute intervals and try to follow the given route closely in an effort to spot *all* the controls, carefully marking each on the map. Missed controls will result in penalty time.

The route should mainly follow terrain features, so map-reading will be used chiefly. Straight lines, where a compass must be used, may also occasionally be incorporated. For beginners, the route should follow big handrail-type features; but, if line orienteering is set up for experienced orienteers, the course should mostly utilize topographic features.

This exercise is mainly a *map-reading* practice.

## SCORE ORIENTEERING

Score orienteering is also a good training event—with emphasis on *route choice*. A special advantage is that the event can be run in a relatively short time-period, perhaps one hour. As you'll recall, score orienteering was described in the *Event* chapter.

## CONTROL PICKING

The idea here is to set a course that offers practice in pinpointing a control from an *attack point*.

Use an area with a lot of small features. The course should be set with no leg exceeding 200 meters and with no leg crossing or being close to any big features, and so that the previously-found control serves as the attack point for the next one.

The time interval between starters must be generous so that they will not be in contact with each other out on the course. Otherwise, the exercise will be spoiled.

With proper course setting on a good detailed map, this exercise may be run without a compass to test the runners' *map-reading* ability.

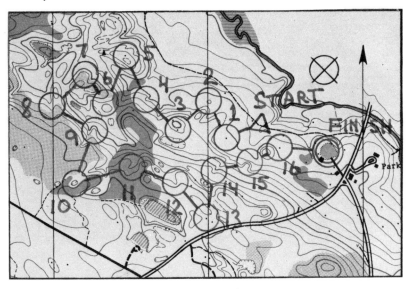

*Control Picking.* Example of a good orienteering *control picking* course— short on big, easy-to-spot features and long on small features. Each control serves as attack point for the next one.

## ROUGH ORIENTEERING

During this exercise, the orienteers will practice the technique of getting themselves as fast as possible to an attack point using either *rough compass* or *rough map-reading*.

The course is laid out with quite long legs and easy controls placed at big features. The legs must be designed so either a straight compass bearing or routes along handrails appear to be the best choices. The controls should be placed very obviously so no time is lost at locating the marker when the feature is reached.

This exercise will give the runners quite a workout on a fairly easy course. Such a course reminds one of a ski orienteering course with easy controls, long legs, and navigation along trails and other handrails.

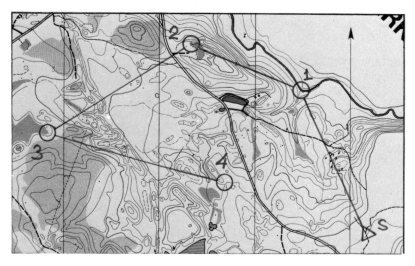

*Rough Orienteering.* The markers for this section of a *rough orienteering* training course are placed at features that normally might be used as attack points.

ASSIGNED ROUTES ORIENTEERING

This exercise offers opportunities to compare different *route choices* between controls against each other. A course of one-half or one-third normal length is set—featuring long legs only; few, and very easy, controls (no time should be spent on finding the markers); and a common start/finish area. Each leg must have two (or possibly three) decent route choices—the routes to be marked on the runners' maps.

The course is first run using the best routes; then, after some rest, completed again via the second-best alternatives. A lively comparison and discussion of the time differences between the runs follows. This will be more interesting if timers were at each control so the times for each leg can be compared.

### BLANK-MAP ORIENTEERING

This is an exercise for practicing *compass-running* and *pacing* skills. The organizer lays out an easy course using big control features. The legs must be short (less than 300 meters), especially for the less advanced groups. Put a blank paper over the area map, trace off the course and the North lines (or use a lined paper). Also, indicate the North end of the map and the scale. This will be the map master to be duplicated. The control descriptions may also be put directly on this map master.

Another way to transfer a course over to blank paper (or maps) is to place the map showing the set course over a paper pad and then put pinholes through the controls to the pad below. Draw the course on the blank sheets using the holes for guidance.

A variation of this exercise is to have maps that are blank except for small areas around the controls where the actual map is shown. This "window orienteering" encourages use of *attack points* and *rough compass*.

The art on the following page shows clearly just how these two rather unorthodox maps are done.

### MAP-MEMORY STAR ORIENTEERING

The aim of this exercise is to practice and improve *map-memory* technique. A starting location is selected in an area from which many handrail-type features lead out. Keeping the starting point in the center, put out a number of very easy controls. Select points that are near handrail features. The only map in use is posted at the start. After the start is signaled, the runner studies the master map and tries to memorize the route to his first control. He then runs out to find the marker. This is a difficult task so the legs must be very easy and quite short. The participants have to return to the start each time they need to look at the map again.

Start: The boulder
1: The knoll
2: The re-entrant,
   upper end
3: The depression
4: The knoll
5: The boulder (2 m),
   west side
6: The re-entrant
7: The boulder
   (2½ m), east side
8: The pit (ø 4 m)

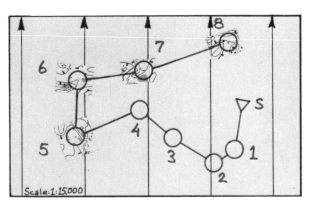

*Combined Blank Map and Window Orienteering.* A section of a good course for *blank map* and *window orienteering* combined. Achieve the "windows" by cutting holes in a plain sheet of paper covering the master map. Draw in the full course and North/South lines before copying, as well as any necessary slope or other terrain clarifications indicated. The full master map is shown below.

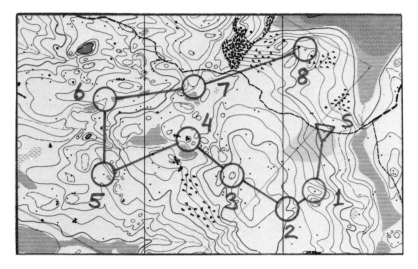

If the participants are not more than the number of controls, a mass start can be used with a different first control for every runner. The runners can then continue to the next marker in a clockwise order. With many participants, a regular staggered start must be used, with generous time spacings.

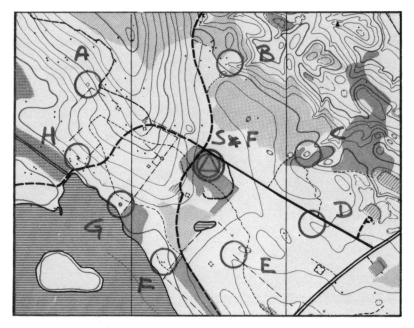

*Star Orienteering.* This training exercise is used to practice map memory. The only map used is the master map which is posted at the Start/Finish area. Although most beginners may find it will take several trys to find even one control without a map, it's OK to visit as many as the memory will allow before returning to the master map.

## CONTROL PLOTTING

If done indoors this exercise offers good training in map-memory; if done outdoors, it also gives good *running* exercise.

A course of appropriate difficulty with approximately ten controls is drawn on a number of master maps. The master maps are placed some distance from the start area. The participants are to copy the course over to their own maps which are kept at the starting location the whole time—requiring them to run back and forth between the start and the master until all the controls are drawn in.

If the exercise is done indoors, it can be made quite exciting by being treated as a relay competition. Outdoors, if the master maps are placed some 100 to 300 meters away from the start (and possibly up a hill), the runners will get a lot of exercise in a short period of time.

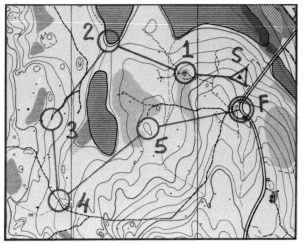

Start: The building
1: The clearing
2: The swamp, so■
   tip
3: The trail end
4: The trail-stream
   crossing
5: The knoll
Finish: The road-tr■
   junction

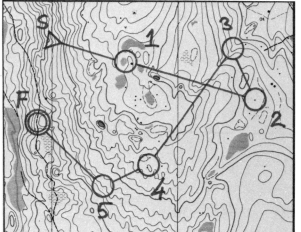

Start: The re-entran■
1: The marsh, east
   edge
2: The boulder
3: The re-entrant,
   lower part
4: The knoll, north
   foot
5: The spur
Finish: The norther■
   trail bend

*Control Plotting.* It is not necessary to give too much thought as to how to connect the controls for these two *control plotting* exercise courses; it is, however, very important that the control features be selected with an eye to the proper degree of difficulty for the participants' skill level—as is true for most exercises. Compare the upper course intended for novices with the one below for experts.

## MINI-ORIENTEERING

This is a good, fun event suitable for relaxed club or group outings.

The organizer draws a very detailed map of the area to be used, with symbols dreamed up for all sorts of objects, such as trees, bushes, lamp posts, etc. A number of controls (the more participants, the more controls) to be taken in any order are then set out and marked with small miniature paper markers (2 to 4 inches) placed at any height level. The markers have code letters that the runners must copy onto their score cards. Have premarked maps available for the runners, and use a mass start. Mayhem rather resembling a scavenger hunt ensues.

Mini-orienteering can also be run indoors, but then ½-inch is a more suitable marker-size. Many other variations on this theme can be arranged; it's up to the imagination of the organizer.

## TRAINING MEETS

Small, informal training meets are probably the most common orienteering training form used. And for good reason: nothing can be closer to the real thing. However, too often they are run very routinely and in familiar areas. To get the most out of a training event, you should keep the following in mind:

1. Don't be competitive. It doesn't matter how you place, as long as you get good practice in different techniques.

2. If you know the area, try to orienteer as if you had never been there before.

3. Always choose a more technically difficult route over a simple running route. Running can be trained another time.

4. Leave your compass at home at times to force yourself into more map-reading.

## COMBI RUNS

All of the practice exercises above can be varied in a lot of ways, or various of them can be combined into a single course to give practice in many of the basic techniques at once, e.g., a combination of compass/pacing lines and route orienteering is perfect for beginners. Which events are combined and how they are arranged is very much up to each organizer's intentions and imagination. However, most of these exercises require a considerable amount of work to plan and set up. If they are not done properly, the value of the training can be lost completely and the work be for naught.

## Physical Training

Orienteering is not a sport for supermen; great speed, strength, or endurance is not required. If you can walk, you can orienteer. But, if you get into orienteering, there comes a time when you sometimes wish you could go faster on the easy stretches of a course. For this, it certainly does help to be in shape.

What can you do to go faster? Maybe what you need—besides map and compass practice—is more old-fashioned exercise between orienteering meets. Unfortunately, the word "exercise" conjures up unhappy images of self-inflicted torture. It doesn't have to be so. Physical training can, and should, be agreeable—sometimes even fun. There is no need to punish yourself; just keep in mind, above all, that you are out for your own enjoyment.

DO'S AND DON'TS

Before you embark on a training program of your own, consider the following:

1. If you have been inactive for several years, see a *doctor* before you begin training. Keep in mind, you ex-athletes, that you cannot accomplish the work that you once could. Take it easy at first! A complete physical exam will get you started on the right foot. A physician can tell you about any limitations you should observe.

2. *Make training a habit.* Whatever you do in preparation for orienteering should be done regularly. Make some form of training part of your daily routine, if possible; just like brushing your teeth.

You will obtain better results by moderate, *regular* training sessions than with occasional weekend exercise "binges."

3. *Train, don't strain.* Your exercise should be in a relaxed, rhythmical and regular form. Coax yourself to adapt gradually to more stress. The human body is a miraculous machine. It will respond to enormous demands of work, but it must be geared up slowly. One half hour to 45 minutes of daily, relatively easy exercise can produce profound changes in one's fitness, but it must be done over a period of weeks, then months. All it takes is a minimum of a half hour daily—that's just one television show you must sacrifice.

4. *Allow time for a brief warm-up and warm-down* before and after each training session. Don't plunge directly into a fast run or bicycle ride. Slowly increase the intensity of any exercise as your body warms up. It's funny how on some days your body responds beautifully, while on others the old engine never does get fully running on all cylinders. Likewise, after a workout, take a couple of minutes to cool off before you take your shower. Don't ask why. Exercise physiologists can't agree on the specific value of warm-ups. But, we know you will feel better—and work better.

5. *Find someone to train with.* Man is a social animal; we all enjoy things more if there is someone else to share them with. Persuade someone else to try orienteering and once he or she is hooked, you have a training partner. Training takes on a more regular pattern when a group of people are involved.

6. *Keep a record.* In a notebook, keep a brief daily log of your training. How far? How fast? How long? How many?—that sort of thing. After a few weeks your improvement will be apparent on paper. Such a notebook could also contain your performances at meets. It is good to get in the habit of writing down where you made your mistakes in a meet. We all can profit from our errors.

7. *Make training fun!* The time that you put aside for training should be a bright spot in your daily routine. Since most of us have relatively sedentary jobs, training should be a welcomed change of pace. Put on those sweat pants and work out. It's the best tranquilizer in the world! Vary the type of exercise so that your training won't get boring. If you are tired of running, go for

a bicycle ride or a walk. Mix up your workouts by changing the scenery as well as the form of exercise. Use a technique training game to get a change.

*Here are some ideas . . .*

Orienteering is closely related to many of the other sports that place similar demands on the cardiovascular system: the lungs, heart, arteries, and veins. So since you rarely can (or would want to) orienteer every day, the next best thing is to train daily using a relative in the cardiovascular family. The following activities are only a few among many that will shape you up for the next orienteering meet:

### WALKING

Just putting one foot in front of the other is an exercise that we seem to have forgotten in this day and age of figure salons and exercise machines and it's still one of the best. Physiologists tell us that there is nothing better than walking to get back in shape, especially if you have let your fitness slip over the last couple of years. So don't forget hiking. If you can get to the mountains, all the better. For practice for walking during weekend orienteering meets, why not walk during the week as well?

If you haven't been out hoofing lately, start your exercise program with a 15 to 20 minute walk—part way to work or home is a good way to begin—or just around the block in the evening. If you are uncomfortable the next day, keep your next few walks of the same duration and distance. As you become accustomed to the physical demands of walking, gradually increase the distance, pace and duration of your daily rambles until you can walk the distance of an orienteering course (5 to 10 kilometers; 3 to 4 miles) without any undo strain. It sounds easy doesn't it? But believe it or not, millions of Americans—adults and children—cannot walk briskly for a half an hour without feeling the consequences, such as sore legs and feet, the next day. When you can accomplish this easily, not only will you be able to orienteer better, you will feel better too.

### R U N N I N G

Advancing beyond walking, a progressively more demanding exercise is running. This is the most common form of training done by orienteers. Since running is more rigorous than walking, you can accomplish a significant workout in considerably less time. As you may know, there is more to running than putting on your sneakers and going out the door: there are several types of running training available to the orienteer. For starters—

Jogging—either alone or combined with other exercise—is excellent conditioning for orienteering.

*Try Some L S D.* Maybe the key to your success in orienteering could be a steady diet of L S D, which stands for "*long, slow, distance*" running. As we mentioned earlier, orienteering is one of the endurance or cardiovascular sports family, and easy, moderate distance running is one of the most efficient tools for developing one's endurance. Running or jogging not only tones the muscles, but more importantly, increases the body's ability to use oxygen, and the more oxygen you can transport to the various muscles, the more work (*i.e.,* running, swimming, skiing) can be done.

How far should you go? Unfortunately, there is no set answer as all of us have different capacities for exercise and are starting at various levels of fitness. But keep in mind some of the ground rules at the beginning of the chapter—especially, "Train, don't strain." If you feel the effects of a particular workout for several days, chances are that you overdid it. Workouts of super-high stress are fine for well-conditioned college athletes, but keep in mind your age and exercise background.

Perhaps the best way for you to begin your "L S D," if you haven't been particularly active for a few years, would be to "walk-run" at first. By alternating periods of walking with a jog, you can increase the benefits of the exercise. Gradually, as you become fitter, the walks take up less and less of the whole workout, as the running portion increases. It is not uncommon for well-conditioned orienteers to run stretches of 8 to 10 miles in a single workout. But bear in mind that they did not start training at such a high level. Also keep in mind that orienteering is done in the woods, so try to train in similar terrain, if you are able. There is a big difference between running on a sidewalk and running through the woods. If you want to learn more on the subject of running and jogging (and about the physiology of exercise in general), look in the bibliography for additional sources of information.

## INTERVAL TRAINING

It doesn't take long to realize that an orienteering meet differs greatly from a conventional foot race. Orienteering probably is more comparable to cross-country skiing than running, in that the physical demands on you are not continuous, but varied. During the course of an orienteering race, there will be some occasions which demand a long continuous run of perhaps a mile, while other times you will be climbing a steep embankment and still other times you will be simply standing still reaching for your map or compass. So, a diet of slow, easy distance running will not by itself completely prepare you for the rigors of a well set orienteering course.

To prepare yourself for orienteering's varied demands, you should occasionally include in your training runs which place varied demands on your body. One such gimmick is called interval training. This device is used by swimmers, runners, cross-country skiers, weight lifters, and oarsmen to improve their performance. And

It takes a good bit of training before orienteers are ready to finish at this pace.

it can be potent medicine to get yourself in shape. *But watch out!!* It can be so potent that it knocks you out of all training for a while with an injury or just very sore muscles—affectionately termed by runners as "rigor-mortis."

Similar to L S D, interval training consists of repeated, fast-paced runs of 100 yards to ¾ of a mile, between which are interspersed recovery periods of walking or relaxed jogging. The interval run should be fast, but not a sprint or all-out effort. As you run one of the "intervals" your body demands more oxygen, and your muscles accumulate waste products of exercise (mostly lactic acid and carbon dioxide) and you get that run-down feeling. During the recovery period, your body tries to adjust to the recently imposed stress. After a sufficient period (scientists say a pulse of 110 to 120 beats per minute indicates you have recovered), you repeat the process again. To help adjust this regimen to your needs, there are four variables which you can manipulate to average the work load to suit your own level best: 1) distance of the interval run; 2) speed or pace of the interval run; 3) length of recovery period; and 4) number of repetitions.

After running a 440-yard run 8 times with a short recovery, you will know that you have accomplished some real work. Such training is not the kind of thing you want to do every day, but during the orienteering pre-season, one interval workout per week will result in greatly improved fitness.


### HILL RUNNING

Another form of interval training, which is used by competitive orienteers and cross-country skiers is repeated runs up a hillside. Ten repeated 100-yard runs can easily be done on a running track, but try doing 100-yard bursts up a grade and you will quickly see what effect gravity has on your movements. As mentioned earlier, orienteering courses rarely cover flat ground; quite the contrary. In most parts of the United States and Canada, you will find many hills as obstacles on the route to a control point.

Like interval training on a track or athletic field, hill running consists of fast runs uphill followed by a recovery walk back down to the bottom. This is a very stressful form of training which should not be done without some fitness background.


### FARTLEK

This variation of interval training originated in Sweden, as did orienteering, and means "speed-play." Of all the forms of interval running we have encountered, *fartlek* appears to be the most appealing and most compatible with the spirit of orienteering. Basically, *fartlek* is an unstructured, free-form interval workout which includes all the previously mentioned forms of training (walking, jogging, L S D, sprinting, hill running, and interval running). The only limitations on the workout are your imagination, time, and energy. With *fartlek*, you can run easily for a while and then throw in a fast quarter-mile effort, followed by more easy running. If you come to a hill, you may rise to the challenge of conquering it with a sprint.

*Fartlek* is best accomplished on rolling terrain such as a golf course or, more ideally, through woods which might approximate an orienteering course. During the course of a 5 to 6 mile *fartlek* run, one would probably begin with an easy jog of 5 to 10 minutes,

Training can be good fun as well as work. Cross-country skiing is an excellent example.

followed by some accelerations over various distances and interspersed with recovery walks or jogs. The run should conclude with a jog to warm-down.

## BICYCLING

Another way of working your cardiovascular system as well as your arms and legs is by bicycling. Bicycling is currently enjoying a comeback as a form of transportation and exercise—and why not? It's fun and even a non-superman can cover a lot of ground on a 10-speed model. But, you can also get in great shape by bicycling. Look at the cross-country ski racers who bicycle so much during the off-season: few people are in better shape than they are.

As a rule of thumb, you should know that it takes about 3 miles of good, hard pedaling to equal one mile of running.

## CROSS-COUNTRY SKIING

Speaking of skiers and their fitness, you might be surprised to know how many people attending orienteering meets cross-country ski in the winter. It makes sense because the two sports have a lot in common. Both take place in the same type of environment, only during different seasons. Both require a varied demand on your cardiovascular system and both foster a great awareness of the outdoors. In fact, the two sports combine in the form of ski-orienteering which is starting to catch on in New England. More can be learned about cross-country skiing in several good books on that subject—once again, see the bibliography.

## There's even more to it . . .

Orienteering training encompasses many activities, as you can see. This chapter only presents a mere smattering of what one can do if interested in becoming a better orienteer. Hopefully, we have gotten across the idea that to get better at orienteering is not just a physical matter, but involves thinking and strategy as well. And perhaps here lies the key to orienteering's wide appeal.

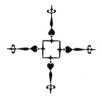

# Course
# Setting

I<small>N ORDER FOR YOU</small> to be able to go orienteering, someone has to set up a meet—get permission to use an area, get or prepare maps, set courses, and run the meet itself. The organization necessary to accomplish this can vary from one man to an extensive club effort. It all depends on the number of participants expected. One person might be able to handle some 20 to 30 people, though even that wouldn't be easy—but above that number more and more manpower must be involved. (See the *Meet Direction* chapter for specific staff requirement guidelines.)

Most participants like to be able to go to a whole series of meets during the year and be in touch with orienteering constantly. To accomplish this a local club, or other interested group, has to be responsible for setting up a schedule and for assigning meet directors for the different meets. With continuity and a program published well in advance, interest in the sport among the participants will be maintained and its spread to other people encouraged.

Most clubs have a policy that all who participate in meets must help with the organization chores now and then. This allows meet organization to remain enjoyable and not become a burden. But independent of the size of the meet, the job is usually broken into three distinct parts: *course-setting, map-making* and *meet direction. Course-setting* is discussed in this first of three chapters on meet organization.

*And It's Fun, Too . . .*

Setting courses for fellow orienteers is an activity many people actually enjoy equally as much as participating in an actual meet. As a course setter, one is on the other side of the fence; instead of solving orienteering problems, you try to create them—interesting and challenging ones. And that makes quite a puzzle for the course setter, too! Then, after a meet the course setter has the chance to compare the routes the runners selected against his/her theoretical intentions: this is always most interesting and often surprising.

## Rules of Thumb

There are a lot of considerations that go into the design of a course, but the main principle is: *create a challenging course with the proper degree of difficulty for the category expected to use it.* This means that the participants should find interesting route choices and orienteering problems in every major part of the course, but always within the general limits of their ability. This fundamental and unique principle of the sport must always be kept in mind and preserved. No dull running legs that allow the orienteer to disconnect his/her mental activity—that's cross-country running and not orienteering.

On the other hand, this shouldn't be overdone. Too great difficulty will just discourage people from further participation. Especially the White course for the rank beginners should be very easy and the requirement of good route choices can be almost neglected. Beginners often find enough problems in just interpreting the map and keeping their directions straight. Take a look at the sample beginner course on the fold-out map.

Another key principle in course-setting is *fairness.* Orienteering should be as exact a sport as possible with all elements of chance eliminated. For the course setter this means very precise work in the field. Important features along all routes must exist in reality—not only on the map. Likewise, aiding or hindering features found in the terrain along the routes must be shown on the map. Maps must be up to date and at the same time any control point with erroneously drawn surroundings must be rejected, etc.

## Setting the Stage

Before you can even think of courses, you have to solve the following complex:

1. Find an area suitable for the categories that will enter the meet, *i.e.*, beginners especially need lots of handrails.

2. Find adequate parking in or adjacent to the area. This choice dictates pretty much where the start and finish must be located. It's best if the finish is next to the parking, or at least near by (less than 500 m.). Also, and less obvious, the finish area should be inviting—people often remain in this area for a long time while their friends or family members come in, or they wait for the results, or maybe have a picnic. The start should also be fairly close or not further than 1 kilometer away.

Solving this particular complex is not always easy, especially when one considers the size of the area necessary and the need for permission from the proper authority. More about site choice follows, but local and state parks make good spots to start the search—and the authorities there are usually most cooperative.

## Course-Setting Basics

The job of setting courses consists of two parts—the first a theoretical one in which the courses are planned on the map only. This is followed by a practical follow up consisting of field checking the theoretical courses for fairness. Often the check will *not* find everything OK and the course-setter must go back to the drawing board to alter the course or update the map. And then again go out in the woods, etc. All this requires a lot of time, so the course-setting job has to be started well ahead of the meet—normally several months or more. However, without time pressure, course-setting can be a very relaxing and enjoyable puzzle, indoors as well as out in the open.

After having selected the parking (these Modern Times!) and finish areas, you can start this course-setting puzzle. And that's exactly what it is because you must fit the following pieces together:

1. Common start and finish areas for all courses.

2. The courses must be of lengths that fit the categories (or class levels) of the participants.

3. Each course must have the correct degree of difficulty.

4. Each leg and each control must have a purpose.

Let's take a closer look at these requirements—and the theory behind them.


ROUTE CHOICE

The main ingredient in orienteering is *route choice*. The controls should be placed in relation to each other so several route alternatives are possible for each leg. Sometimes this is not feasible on every leg but these dull legs must be made as short as possible—and as few. Some of the most important factors to consider in plotting good route choice follow:

*Avoiding Lost Distance.* A general principle used to set up route choices is to discourage the straight-on approach. Place the controls so major obstacles, like swamps, hills, etc.—or better, a complex of them—fall in the bee line. However, watch out that the obstacle does not act as a collecting feature instead and create a "lost distance" situation—"lost distance" meaning that a big collecting feature is found right before a control, allowing the runners to go full speed shooting for (or zeroing in on) this "collector" without being exposed to orienteering problems on that stretch. It might as well have been a X-C race—the *distance is lost* from the viewpoint of learning about orienteering. Linear features (trails, streams, etc.) are especially bad to have before a control. But place the marker before, let's say the trail, instead, and you wouldn't have any problem. See controls 9 and 11 on the Blue course on the fold-out map. Strangely enough, if there are no attack points along the trail, it will not matter much. The runner will perhaps be helped with distance but not with direction. The Blue leg 6–7 shows an example.

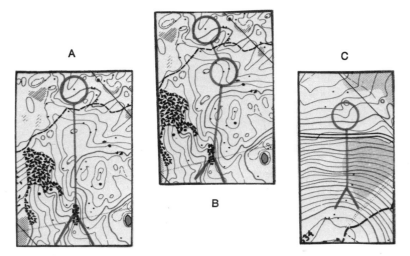

*Lost Distance.* Leg A gives a good example of lost distance—plain running without true orienteering. All the leg requires is to follow a compass bearing to the trail, then picking up an attack point along the trail from which it would only be 100 meters in to the control. In Leg B the lost distance is avoided by inserting a control just *before* the handrail (trail)—a typical course setters' technique. C shows that handrails without check points along them do not necessarily create lost distance. The orienteer will be aided in keeping track of his distance but not of his direction.

*Avoiding Dog Legs.* Sometimes you also have to plan controls for other reasons than route creation. This is to avoid a dog leg, or in other words, a situation in which runners coming in towards a control will see and be aided unfairly by the orienteers leaving the marker ahead of them. To avoid this it is necessary to turn the "leavers" away from the "comers." These direction-changing legs are naturally kept as short as possible.

Summing up: a control—and the course-setting it represents—must be justified by one of the following reasons:

1. To produce a good leg with several interesting route choices.

2. To enable the next leg to be a good one.

3. To avoid a dog leg.

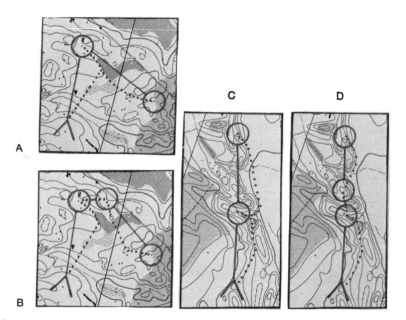

*Dog Legs.* Formation of dog legs—a course allowing the control "comers" to see the "leavers"—depends more on the terrain surrounding the control than on the shape of the legs themselves. In A, it is the marsh—serving as a collecting feature and handrail for both incoming and outgoing runners—that causes the dog leg. A direction-changing control, as in B, solves the problem.

Although both legs in C are clearly separate, the route choices created by the topography create a dog-leg problem nonetheless. An additional control (in D) eliminates the unwanted outgoing route choice—and the dog leg.

*Course Length.* It's important and quite evident that the course setter must keep the lengths of the courses within the established limits. Distances for standard courses are suggested in the *Event* chapter. Most orienteers will not get full satisfaction and a feeling of accomplishment if the course is too short. On the other hand, on an overlong course, the meet organizer might well have to go out and retrieve overtired participants. The terrain type and how fast it is to run through are other factors to take into account when making a final decision on course lengths.

*Degree of Difficulty.* As we have said, the difficulty of the various "suggested" routes as well as the controls themselves must be on a par with the runners—neither too hard nor too easy for them. The number of collecting and handrail features determine how difficult an area will be. To make a beginner's course easy enough the course is set so they can follow along handrails most of the time from control to control. The route choices are not very important for beginners: they find it enough challenge just to read the map and head in the right direction. Note the fold-out map's White course. However, advanced courses can also be set through the same area as the beginner's course by directing the runners' route choices *across* the handrails instead of along them. In this way, they get little help from them. This is especially true if there are no distinct features along the handrail where the course crosses; otherwise you may get *lost distance.*

## CONTROL PLACEMENT

Control placement must also vary between the various courses. Again, beginner's controls must be easy. But what determines the difficulty of a control? These are the key factors:

1. *Size* of the control feature.

2. *Distance* from possible attack points. Novice controls must be on or very near a handrail.

3. *Placement* on the feature itself; for example, control location for beginners should be "*top* of the knoll" but for advanced "*foot* of the knoll."

4. *Height* the marker is placed above the ground. Control flags for advanced runners may be placed quite low and not be visible until you stand on the control feature, but novice controls should be discoverable from a distance (at least 20 to 25 meters).

5. Perhaps chief among all control placement considerations is that all controls must be *distinct* and *fair.* Control definitions like "the hillside" or "the valley" are features too vague to be used. Likewise are non-map features like "a log" or "a tree stump."

Fairness also dictates that nothing be allowed to require more than what is possible. This applies to control placement as well as to course-setting in general. For example, even good orienteers don't have better than ±3° precision (or 10 percent of covered distance) when running on a compass bearing. So control features should have a collecting front (including the distance from which they can be seen) of better than 10 percent of the distance from the nearest possible attack point. To hit objects smaller than that (e.g., markers hidden in small pits or foundations) requires good luck and is gambling—not orienteering.

### MORE BASICS

Try to make the courses interesting and a good test of all the participants' skills. Let them run through different types of terrain. Have different types of control features. Also vary, if possible, the lengths of the legs and their directions to make the courses further interesting and attractive.

Sometimes the same control can be used by more than one course. And this is especially acceptable if the easiest course approaches the control from the easy side and the more advanced course from another direction. But watch out that you don't create a dog-leg at the same time. Common legs should exist only on rare occasions.

*Always pay attention to the safety of the runners.* Don't run the course across a big dangerous cliff or force the runner to wade swift or deep streams. And there are many other don'ts. Safety considerations should be kept in mind throughout.

Preserve good relations with landowners by avoiding private or sensitive areas. Such areas should be marked on the map with a cross-screen indicating "prohibited area" if it's at all possible that some runner might plan to run through it. Naturally all fields with crops must not be trespassed. Plan the courses accordingly.

Finally, the legs from the last controls in to the finish should be coordinated so the runners can approach the finish from only one direction. This makes life easier and more pleasant for the officials at the finish as well as for the spectators. If this is difficult to accomplish, you can guide the finishers in by using streamers

*The Finish.* An example of a good finish: short finish legs, runners arriving from one direction only and with the finish itself easily seen from a good distance. To be sure that the runners from control C approach from the desired direction, streamers should be put to guide them. The three course descriptions would end as follows:

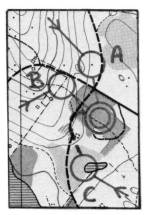

A (AC) The boulder (2 m), southeast side
Finish: In the field

---

B (FD) The path-stone wall crossing
Finish: In the field

---

C (LP) The swamp, west edge
Finish: Follow blue-yellow streamers

from the last control in; here again, as shown on the fold-out map. But make this area short if you have to have one—we want as much orienteering and as little X-C racing as possible.

## SOME PRACTICAL TIPS

Some more practical how-to tips may be welcome among all this theory. When working out a course-setting puzzle, it's very handy to have a map palette. This consists of a stiff board with the map taped to it. Over the map is fastened a sheet of fairly thick clear plastic (drafting film can also be used). In this way the courses can be sketched out on the film and still leave a clean map available if erasures are necessary on the film as the work progresses. Wax (grease) pencils, or special felt-tip pens used with overhead projectors, can be used to draw on the film. Deletion is done with a piece of cloth. If the map is fastened on one edge only and several plastic films fastened at the other edge, several courses can be worked on simultaneously. Course-setters should get in the habit of taking their map palettes along whenever there might be some spare minutes. (See next page.)

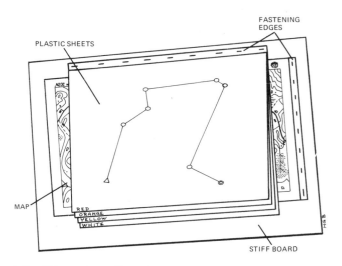

*Map palette.* This system allows the course setter to always have access to a fresh map. The plotting is done on films which easily can be wiped clean—a real advantage. When working on a particular course the area map is folded in under that particular film; with the map in the bottom position, it's possible to see the interaction between all courses—another real advantage.

## The Field Check

Course-setting is as much outdoors work as theoretical figuring. A lot of field checking and probably redesigning must be done. Armchair courses are not permitted.

### THINGS TO CHECK

Every control must be checked and be accurate from all realistic attack points, which also have to be correct. In addition, the immediate area around a control has to agree with the map. If any discrepancies are found the course-setter must either update the map or move the control. The course-setter must naturally be skilled in using the compass and also at pacing to be able to locate a control exactly. A sighting compass is also of good help. Remember: to be fair, the expanse of the visible front of the control feature must be at least 10 percent of the distance from the feature to the nearest reasonable attack point.

Likewise it must be verified that handrails and collecting features along the possible route choices do exist and are correctly drawn. If, for example, a trail shown on the map tapers off into nothing, it's most unfair for the runners who have based their routes on that trail. Logging can create such tricks even on new, accurate maps. Especially any new area must be gone over carefully and this will take time. Also, any very dense and slow areas along routes come across during the field checking should be shown for the participants—maybe through a map correction they can add themselves. Fight for fairness.

Any areas or objects that might jeopardize the safety of the participants should be indicated on the map or by map corrections. For example, dangerous pits, quarries, cliffs, and barbed wire belong in this category. If these safety hazards are near a control or right on the track where many people are likely to pass, they should be marked by red and yellow streamers as warning. Be especially safety conscious at night courses. Flag danger areas by white streamers then. If it's practical, the course-setter can do this course marking at the time of the field check; otherwise, the meet director should attend to this just prior to the meet.

**Course setters in the field.**

As we have said before, other areas that must be made known to the participants by being marked on the map or through map corrections are prohibited areas. These areas can be private land, sensitive areas (young forest, wild life), etc. Naturally all fields with crops also belong in this category and must not be trespassed. This is one of the fundamental ethical codes of orienteering. In some cases it is also a good idea to flag prohibited areas by red/yellow streamers. Everything possible should be done to preserve good relationships with the land managers.

### SETTING OUT THE FLAGS

When it is decided that the planned control locations are good and fair and the course-setter has checked all the possible routes in to the control, the control place itself—and is satisfied that everything is accurate—it's time to set out the marker itself. Or, at least, to mark where the flag is to be placed.

The control points are of course checked out well before the meet, but the flags themselves are put out just before the meet— either in the morning of the meet day or possibly the afternoon before. This is to avoid vandalism or perhaps wind, or other, damage. During the field check the location is marked with a piece of weatherproof streamer (fabric) and an identification number. This number may be written in permanent ink on the streamer itself, or better yet, on a tag hung next to the streamer. At control-marker hanging time, the tags should be retrieved to verify that all the controls have been placed. At this point it is especially useful if the course-setter has helpers to set out the flags.

But, first, some thought must go into exactly where to place the flag. As we have seen the difficulty of the control can be varied depending upon where and how high the marker is placed. The height can vary from chest-high for beginners to nearly touching the ground for experts. But it's more a matter of visibility around the control. The marker must always be visible if you stand on the control feature described in the control definitions. It must not be hidden behind trees, bushes, etc.; we want orienteering—not a treasure hunt. Novice controls should be visible from a good distance (more than 25 meters) but expert markers can be more secluded (5 meters). These are naturally relative figures; it all depends upon how well defined the control feature itself is. On rare occasions streamers may be put up to make the control easier to find—although, normally, any control that difficult to find would have been rejected in the first place. But, if this is done, be sure it is indicated in the control descriptions.

When marking a control, it should be checked from different directions and the streamer placed exactly where the marker is wanted. Its lower end should be hung where the lower part of the marker is to be. This makes it easy to place the markers just prior to the meet. It can be checked with an actual marker before the ribbon is placed if there is doubt. Account should be taken of how the vegetation and the visibility will be at the day of the meet. Then, after each streamer is placed, the control should be marked on the map, together with its number, and then this information—plus the appropriate control description—written down on a piece of paper. This helps keep track of the marked-out controls.

## The Control Descriptions

After all points are finalized, it's time for paper work again. Master maps must be drawn for all courses and control descriptions written for them. These should be as *brief* but also as *precise* as possible.

A recommended form is: control number, control code (within parentheses), the feature (plus dimensions and identifying clarification if needed), where on the feature, and additional information if required. A feature shown on the map is defined with the definite article "the," while an unmarked object has the indefinite article "a." The *Start* and *Finish* should also be described. The course, or class, designation and course length make up a heading for the description slip. Included at the bottom are the maximum time, safety bearing to nearest road, and a reminder to return the control card and to report back to the finish.

The following and the examples on the fold-out map will give you a good idea:

*Yellow Course 4.2 km*

Start: The knoll

1  (51)  The boulder (2.5 m), west side

2  (52)  The path-ditch crossing. Barbed wire west of control

3  (53)  The cliff foot (3 m), south end. Water stop

4  (23)  The western pit (4 m)

5  (55)  A spring

Finish: Follow streamers 200 m

Maximum time: 3 hours

Safety bearing: due west

ALWAYS return your control card or report to finish!

# The Master Maps

The master maps must be drawn with the *highest possible* accuracy and with the control location in the dead center of the control ring. The control circle should be approximately 6 mm (¼ inch) in diameter. The start is marked by a triangle with about 7 mm sides and the finish by two concentric circles (7 and 5 mm). The points of the course should be interconnected by straight lines from the start via the controls to the finish. If the leg from the last control to the finish is marked by streamers, show this route by a dashed line on the master map. The controls should also be numbered.

The recommended color for marking maps is a red/purple color which is easy to see—even for most color blind people. Use a waterproof pen (e.g., a ball point pen).

# Special Situations

Just a couple of words about two somewhat special and different course types—*Night-O* and *Ski-O*. And a word about course-setting competitions for the really dedicated.

## NIGHT-O

Course-setting for Night-O is quite similar to that for regular day orienteering but the course should be routed through a more cultivated area with many handrails and man-made features, creating lots of route choices. Pure woods courses are too hard. Route choices along handrails are favored because of the slowness of running through the woods in the dark. Special attention must be paid to the safety of the runners—no cliffs, or other danger areas are permitted. Remember that the runners can't see that well from just a lamp.

*Night-O Control.* Normally night-O controls are marked with battery-powered lanterns with red 360-degree lenses—the power coming from a single "D" cell, with a low-wattage bulb (1.5 volts/ 0.1-0.2 amp.). For smaller meets, reflector markers may be adequate. These can be made of wood or 1-inch plastic rod wrapped with reflective tape. These markers are harder to find but are simpler and cheaper—and never run out of power.

## SKI-O

Ski-O, on the other hand, is totally based on route choices, mainly along roads and trails. It seldom pays for a skier to go cross-country on a compass bearing . . . it just helps the next person and it's a lot of work. The markers must be located right on trails or tracks and should not present any problems in finding them. The best Ski-O area is a cultivated area with lots of roads, trails, and possibly fields and lakes. The legs are, as a rule, very long—to include as many route combinations as possible. A Ski-O course is normally twice as long as a corresponding foot-O course. To avoid dog-legs, extra controls may be inserted creating some short legs.

The course setter can also create new routes by incorporating ski or skimobile tracks. But it's often quite difficult to set them exactly where they are wanted in winter conditions. The *start* and *finish* points should be marked with streamers to avoid confusion with other tracks in the area. Also, put out streamers at intersections with other tracks. These auxiliary tracks must be marked on the maps with a dashed line.

Fairness is the rule here too. To ensure fairness the conditions of the roads and trails also must be shown on the map. Sanded or snow-free roads or trails should be crossed over. Trails and roads without tracks are marked with cross bars. The organizer must ensure that all other relevant roads and trails have ski or skimobile tracks and are skiable. All this additional information may be drawn on the maps by the organizer or by the participants themselves using map correction masters.

A regular staggered start is used at Ski-O's, but if a heavy snow fall has covered all the tracks the organizer has painfully set out, it's more fair to use a mass start. And, by the way, running is permitted on Ski-O's as long as the runner carries all his ski equipment along.

### COURSE-SETTING COMPETITIONS

Enthusiastic course-setters can put all this theoretical course-setting information to the test with advantage at course-setters competitions. At these, competitors receive a map, plus rules and stipulations giving category, distance, etc. From the returned maps, after a reasonable time a jury normally selects the theoretically best course based in general on the amount and quality of the route choices. Deductions are made for lost distances, dog-legs, etc.

Information as to the time and location of these competitions can usually be obtained from similarly interested orienteers and certainly through the national Federation.

## Summing Up

A final word on course-setting: it's very valuable for all types of orienteering courses to let somebody test-run the courses if at all possible. Valuable feedback and critique is obtained that way. Especially, it will reveal if the course-setter's judgment of terrain difficulty and course length resulted in an appropriate finishing time.

All this design, checking, changes, re-checking, etc., will take quite a few weekends, so be sure enough time is available. Course-setting will then become a fine and very enjoyable recreational activity, in addition to being the integral part of orienteering it always is.

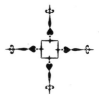

# Map
# Making

THE MAP IS THE MOST important tool of orienteering. Unfortunately, as we have said before, very few standard maps are accurate enough to satisfy the requirements of orienteers. To make the choice among all the possible routes fair and not dependent on chance, all main features must be shown. Otherwise orienteering turns into a gamble instead of a contest of skills—the focal idea behind the sport. Therefore, at least all man-made features (roads, trails, buildings), all prominent hydrographic features (lakes, streams, swamps), and all major topographic features (hills, valleys, cliffs, etc.), should be shown. The man-made category especially often suffers from discrepancies on the map.

One reason for inaccurate maps is that the information on maps of populated areas becomes outdated quite fast. Just in the time it takes to produce an official map, many man-made features may change. This is not too surprising when one realizes that this time —the time from taking the necessary aerial photos until the time one can buy the map from a retailer—is typically three years. Also, on most modern maps very little time is spent on field checking. Features that are easy to misinterpret from aerial photos—trails, for instance—are rarely verified, and sometimes totally erroneous.

The experienced orienteers are the ones who appreciate a good map most, though it is actually the novices who need it most— without experience they tend to get confused easily, and even lost, if features are missing. And when this happens, they often never show up for another meet. So, to make orienteering a success in

Map-maker taking a sighting down a stone wall. Carefully prepared maps are essential to successful orienteering.

your area, someone will probably have to tackle the job of updating and producing better maps. The job can make an excellent club project and should be on every club's program. The club's meet organizers will certainly find it most rewarding to be able to invite fellow orienteers to runs on better and better maps.

But don't be fooled. To produce entirely corrected and field-checked maps in color is a major task. On the other hand, if your goal is simply to check out (and properly pinpoint) the buildings, roads, trails and fields in a smaller area on an already existing map, it's a quite reasonable project. A very rough time guideline is one day's work per square kilometer, although this naturally varies greatly depending on the number of trails, map quality, personal character, etc. Many orienteers consider map-making a highly enjoyable spin-off from orienteering and are eager to venture into the woods at almost any time to check out a map, or to create a new one by finding the problems and figuring out how to show them correctly on the map. Others don't.

A valuable extra dividend from field-checking and map-making is that it trains the map-maker or map-checker to become a more proficient map reader and thereby a better orienteer. This chapter is designed to give the reader an idea of what is involved in map-making and field-checking. For those in your club interested in map-making, it should be a must. But all will learn more about orienteering from even casual attention to the basic map-making procedures outlined here.

## Map Scale

As we saw in the *Map & Compass* chapter, there are several scales used for orienteering maps. The most common are: 1:25,000, 1:20,000, 1:15,000 and 1:10,000. It really doesn't matter which scale your club settles for. Orienteers very soon get used to running on maps of various scales. The best plan is to pick a scale so the finished map fits on a standard paper size (*i.e.*, 8½″ x 11″ or 11″ x 14″). If the map has a lot of detail, select a scale large enough to permit reproduction without making the printed map cluttered. (1:15,000 is a convenient scale in most cases.) Teaching maps covering small areas, e.g., schools or urban parks, might well be printed in even larger scales, such as 1:5,000, 1:2,000, or possibly 1:1,000.

## Basic Procedure

Making maps normally consists of the following basic steps:

1. *Locating an area suitable for orienteering*—an area a minimum of 1 to 2 square kilometers. Getting permission to map and use the area.

2. *Finding the best maps* of the area and from these creating a base map. Making field-work copies.

3. *Field-checking the area.* This is the most time consuming part, but also very enjoyable. Figure on 5 to 40 hours per sq. km., depending on goals, map quality and skills.

4. *Drafting.* This involves either putting the corrections on the master map or drawing an entirely new master and should include *magnetic* North lines and a legend.

5. *Printing the final map.*

## Map-making Methods

There are several ways to generate new maps. Here are some approaches, listed in order of sophistication. The simplest ones are apt to give very crude results and should be used only at small events (less than 20 to 30 participants). One of the more advanced methods will give much better results. But limit the field-checking for the first attempt to major features only to make the project less time-consuming. *Note:* The individual steps are more specifically described after the methods.

METHOD 1 : WORKING IN FINAL
( MASTER MAP ) SCALE

*Step 1.* Draw the magnetic north lines on the original map.

*Step 2.* Make field-check copies.

*Step 3.* Field check.

*Step 4.* Transfer the corrections directly onto the original map.

*Step 5.* Include text, scale and legend.

*Step 6.* Make copies with any copy machine that gives good prints.

This method gives quite a crude result because the corrections are made in scale on a paper that is hard to correct. But it is a quick way: copies can be obtained while one waits from most copying facilities.

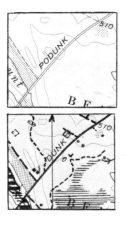

**Method 1.**

*At top,* the uncorrected map section. The amount of detail shown is limited. (On a standard topographical map, the plain area here would show as light green—or dense woods.)

*Below,* the map has been field checked and corrected according to Method 1. Corrections are made with an eraser knife and a fine-point black ballpoint pen. An LT-36 screen has been used to show cleared areas.

Scale: 1:24,000

If the scale is smaller than 1:25,000 a photographic blow-up should be made, e.g., to 1:15,000, to make the final map more legible and the corrections more precise. Actually even 1:24,000/1:25,000 maps also will improve substantially if they are enlarged first. If the original map has green color for woods, this green can be filtered away at the time of enlargement; in this way the final copied maps will come out much clearer.

## METHOD 2: ENLARGEMENT TO 2X FINAL SCALE ONTO WASH-OFF DRAFTING FILM

*Step 1.* Photo-enlarge the particular area of the base map onto wash-off drafting film 2x final scale.

*Step 2.* Erase off all unwanted, disturbing names and details.

*Step 3.* Draw the *magnetic* North lines on the wash-off master (with spacing two times too large).

*Step 4.* Make field-check copies in scale.

*Step 5.* Field-check and transfer the corrections to the wash-off master.

*Step 6.* Include text, legend and scale.

*Step 7.* Print maps (offset) with a scale reduction to 50 percent.

This method produces excellent copies without much drafting work. The reduction makes the drafting crisp and clear and covers minor drafting problems. However, the details carried over from the original map will be disturbingly fat if the new map is a substantial enlargement of the original map.

**Method 2.** To produce this map using Method 2, corrections are done in drafting pencil and with rub-on screens. All names have been removed and the amount of detail is far greater than in the Method 1 example.

Scale: 1:15,000

### METHOD 3: ENLARGE TO 2X FINAL SCALE AND RETRACE

Step 1. Enlarge the particular area of the base map to be used to two times the final scale desired.

Step 2. Draw in the magnetic North lines.

Step 3. Make field-check copies in scale.

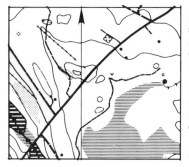

**Method 3.** Based on the black and white symbol list in the appendix, ink pens and screens have been employed to produce this map using the Method 3 technique.

Compare this map against the corresponding area of the fold-out color map. Color helps greatly to make the map easier to read and interpret, especially in the crowded areas.

Scale: 1:15,000

*Step 4.* Draw double-spaced *magnetic North* lines on a drafting film which will be the new master.

*Step 5.* Field-check and transfer both corrections and all unchanged details over to the drafting film master.

*Step 6.* Include text, legend and scale.

*Step 7.* Print maps (offset) with a scale reduction to 50 percent.

The above method produces the best looking copies but requires more drafting work than the previous methods.

METHOD 4: NEW BASE MAP IN 2X
FINAL SCALE FROM AERIAL PHOTOS
PRINTED IN COLOR

*Step 1.* Obtain aerial photos of the area to be used in the form of positive film for viewing in stereo plotting instruments. The pictures must have an overlap of about two-thirds to get stereoscopic coverage.

*Step 2.* Have a mapping company specialized in orienteering maps produce a topographic base map two times the desired final scale. Get several copies if possible.

*Step 3.* Make field-check copies as needed.

*Step 4.* Field-check and transfer any corrections as well as unchanged details over to the drafting film master.

*Step 5.* Draw separate masters for each color.

*Step 6.* Print in color with a scale reduction to 50 percent.

This gives the ultimate in orienteering maps, but it will cost some money. The base map will probably cost $50 to $150 per square kilometer. Companies specializing in O-maps will produce superior base maps. Their operators include all details that orienteers are interested in and the first-class base map will reduce the field-check time substantially. Unfortunately, chances are that your club will have to contact a Scandinavian company to find such specialists.

Also, the color printing is expensive, especially as map printing requires a high-quality press. The map could, of course, go black and white, but that's a pity on such a good base.

*Let' go back to basics . . .*

# The Base Map

## MAP SOURCES

The first place to check to find suitable maps is the local book and/or sporting goods store. It is likely that they will have the best available maps right there. But, if nothing there is of decent accuracy, don't give up. Other local sources of good maps often exist and are worth looking into. Some towns have mapped their land for planning purposes; towns or counties also often have good wetland maps. Areas where major construction projects have been discussed have often been mapped in a very detailed way. Local survey companies can probably offer hints and aid.

If all local sources fail, there is still the national government. Information on United States and Canadian map sources was given at the beginning of the *Map & Compass* chapter. Check there or in the appendix. In the U.S., maps of the following larger scales exist: 1:24,000 (7½-minute series), 1:62,500 (15-minute series), and 1:63,360 (Alaska). (The "minute" term comes from how big a part of the globe [figured in "minutes"] the map covers latitude/longitude-wise—a "minute" being $\frac{1}{60}$th of a degree.) The better Canadian maps come in 1:25,000 or 1:50,000 scales. The contour interval (lines indicating elevation increases and decreases) varies greatly from map to map, from 5 to 100 feet, depending on the topography of the area.

*Aerial Photos.* Aerial photos can be of considerable help, although probably not as much as one might expect. They can show a number of new reference points, but are quite hard to interpret. There is, however, as we have seen, one great use for aerial photos —for producing new, and also very accurate, base maps. (See under mapping Method 4 above.) To be useful, the photos must be taken when the trees have a minimum of obscuring leaves. Early spring is best, when the sun is high and shadows quite short.

The appendix lists sources of aerial photos, but anyone looking for aerial maps can also check local surveying companies for help.

## MAP ENLARGEMENTS

The simplest way to get high-quality enlargements made is to go to a photo-copying (or blueprint) company. They are accustomed to handling jobs of this nature. Also, they can prepare the enlargements on water erasable mylar (wash-off) film, which is easy to correct. The approximate cost is $5. per square foot enlargement. But, if the map-makers in your club don't mind retracing all the details or working with a harder-to-correct master map, most any commercial photographer (advanced amateurs, too) can supply an adequate enlargement on paper. This is quite a bit cheaper. Advertising art and layout companies might also supply such enlargements using a photostat camera.

Whoever makes the enlargements, the area on the map to be blown up should be specified by drawing a frame around it. At the same time the distance between two marks (or a side of the frame) can be used to show to what size the map should be enlarged. If the map has a color for the wooded areas (green) ask the enlarger to filter away that color to get better contrast on the other details. But first thin black lines should be drawn around all fields or clearings; otherwise, these boundaries will be lost.

## MAGNETIC-NORTH LINES

Before the field-check copies of the base map are made the *magnetic-North lines* must be included. The declination information provided on the map or on official maps of the same area is normally sufficient. Draw in the lines as accurately as possible. If the information is very old—the rate of change is in general less than 1° per 10 years—you should try to obtain more recent data. The magnetic North may also be figured from an accurate bearing taken with a sighting compass between two well defined landmarks in your area. We saw how to do this in the *Map & Compass* chapter.

If the base map is going to be retraced, the North lines can be spaced out so they will be handy to use together with the compass —about an inch apart is good. If the lines are to be drawn on a master map that is going to be printed, it's preferable that they are drawn some even distance apart. Then the North lines can be used to help judge distance. However, this distance must correspond to a maximum of 30 mm spacing on the final map; otherwise, the lines will not always lay under the compass. Spacing of one line on the map for every 500 meters in the field is recommended for maps in the scales of 1:15,000, 1:20,000 and 1:25,000.

Just which direction North is on the North lines can be shown with the help of arrows drawn in at both ends of the lines. These arrows make it easier to orient the map properly.

## Field Checking

### FIELD-WORK COPIES

Several field-work copies of the base map are needed before the field work can start. A problem to be aware of: many copy methods distort and change the dimensions of the copy as compared to the original. Paper copies also change dimensions noticeably depending on the humidity.

It is best to let a photo-copying (or blueprint) company make copies on a medium they recommend as stable without being too expensive.

### FIELD-CHECKING MAP BOARD

Another must before the field work can start is a map board—or rather, at least one. This consists of a light weight board of about 12 x 15 inches in size. The best materials are door skin or paneling plywood, or better yet Plexiglas, which can also be used as a portable light table.

Once the board is set, a piece of the field-work map copy is taped on top of the board. This is then covered with drafting film

*Map-maker and map board at work.* Both the orienteering and more sophisticated sighting compass this map-maker carries along will come in handy—as will the ample supply of pens.

taped to the board with waterproof tape—get a mechanical pencil with water- and smear-proof drafting leads (available in assorted colors, too)—and Eureka! the field-working can proceed independent of the weather. Be it sunshine, rain or snow—one can still write on the film. This is definitely impossible with a paper copy.

## PROPER PROCEDURE

Basically field-checking work consists of locating fixed reference points from which the proper directions and distances to features not accurately mapped can be measured. These measurements are then transferred to the map board and gradually all the missing features are drawn in. Good base maps with lots of reference points will make the job a lot easier.

The best season for field work is when there are the fewest leaves on the trees and bushes. The good visibility makes it much easier to determine positions, find features worth mapping, and see the lay of the land. The lack of bugs then makes the job really pleasant, too.

*Taking Bearings.* A regular compass (bigger model) might be used to take bearings, but not for distances exceeding 200 meters. For any sighting longer than 50 meters at least two readings should be taken and then averaged. Sighting compasses can be used over longer distances without multiple readings and are recommended. To transfer the bearing to the map board, use any protractor compass or a separate protractor.

*Figuring Distance.* Distance measurements are done by pacing, using a measuring scale graduated in paces (see the *Technique* chapter for a quick refresher on how to prepare these). The checker should make it a habit to estimate the distance *before* pacing (if estimating in meters the measuring scale must have meters too). After some time it is possible to just estimate most distances shorter than 30 meters and be very accurate.

*In the Field.* The first phase of the field work consists of mapping all roads and trails in the area. These will serve as a reference network for the future mapping. At the same time, houses and other objects that can be seen from the roads and trails should be included. For this work, visibility doesn't matter much, so it can be done any time of the year. Next come the fields, clearings, and major hydrographic features (streams, ponds, bigger marshes). The area then mapped would be adequate enough for beginners and smaller meets. For a first-time mapper, this is a recommended goal.

*But*, if the aim is to have the entire area mapped accurately, there has to be a systematic search through the areas between the handrails (or obvious guidelines). Cliffs, boulders, marshes, knolls, etc., should also be included. If time and ability permit, this is the time to adjust contours and add intermediate form contours—a difficult and time-consuming job (intermediate form contours are used to show minor elevation changes that do not intercept a regular interval contour—i.e., small knolls, spurs, re-entrants, etc.). But it is these refinements which make the map *show* what an orienteer *sees*—he isn't fixed to any set contour intervals.

Documenting the corrections in the field can be done in black lead only. But if several color leads are used, it will be much easier to keep track of the changes made. A good color scheme is: red—contours; blue—hydrographic features; black—man-made and rock features; and finally, green—open areas. Purple can be used to indicate features and lines to be deleted. By the way, an emery board (for fingernails) makes an excellent in-the-field pencil sharpener.

To get the best possible results from field-checking, the checker should discipline himself to transfer each day's corrections to the master map at the end of each field-check session. There are nearly always some details that don't get noted correctly on the map board, but are kept correctly in mind. This memory bank should be tapped right away. As we all know, it's very easy to forget all too quickly.

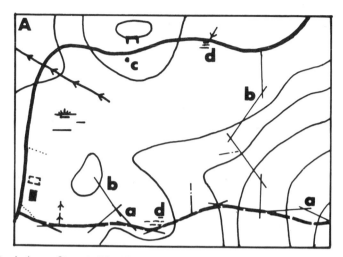

*Mapping technique. Step 1* (A): After getting a feeling of the area to be mapped by walking through it, verify the established trails (a) and lay in all non-marked trails (b). At the same time plot all possible objects near the trails, *e.g.,* the boulder (c), and indicate features that should be included but reach away from the trails, the swamps (d) for example. (A reminder: most map-makers will be thoroughly conversant with map terminology and symbols by the time they arrive at actually mapping, but the reference lists of map symbols in the appendix and on the fold-out map should not be forgotten.)

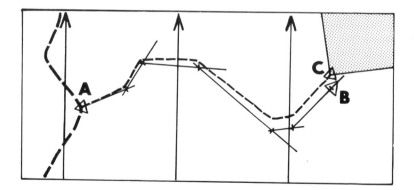

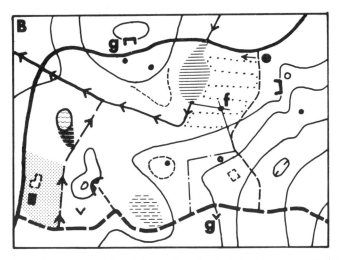

*Step 2* (B): Complete plotting all indicated features. Search the areas between the plotted features to find all other objects worth mapping. In flat
areas a systematic search may be necessary (e); streamers can be useful
to mark out extra reference points. Compass sightings (from at least two
points is recommended) and distance measurements should be used to
plot these newly determined features. When finishing the final drawing
ample room should be left between symbols to help insure good legibility.
B also shows well the use of identifying screening.

---

*Linear features.* As shown at left, linear features are laid in by taking a
compass sighting along the feature as far as it is possible to see from
a fixed start point (A). Plot the bearing on the map; pace count the distance to the end point and transfer it to the map. Take a new bearing from
that point, and so on, until the entire feature (road, trail, ditch or whatever) is plotted.

Even with care, there is often a closing error when executing this technique, *i.e.,* the plotted line (B) doesn't end exactly where the actual feature
reaches (C). If the error is more than 10 percent of the distance or 10° in
bearing, the feature should be resurveyed in the reverse direction. For
smaller errors, simply reposition the plot by gradually moving all points
on the line a proportionately decreasing distance as it approaches the
start point. The trail A–C, at left, is a reposition of the plot A–B.

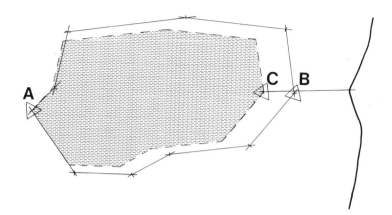

*Plotting larger areas.* The method pictured above is used to plot features covering a largish flat area (swamps, clearings, hill bases, etc.). The fact that the surveyed loop closes doesn't always mean that the plot is accurate. The furthermost point of the plot (B) should be checked against a new fix point; a repositioning may be necessary (C).

*The contour lines.* Contour lines on a topographic map connect points with equal elevation above sea level. This information itself does not help the orienteer sufficiently. For one thing, the small features between the contours do not show. The orienteer wants the map to show what he can expect to see ahead of him. The map-maker can help in this by adding intermediate form contours around various features. In the above illustration, summit A, high area B, small knoll C and the spur E are examples of this. Features that do not intersect a main contour may also be shown as long as the feature is near the line or is well pronounced, *i.e.,* re-entrants or the knoll D above. A contour line may vary ± half a contour interval. However, remember that changing contours is a difficult and time consuming task.

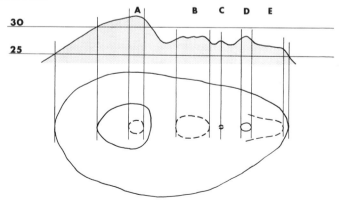

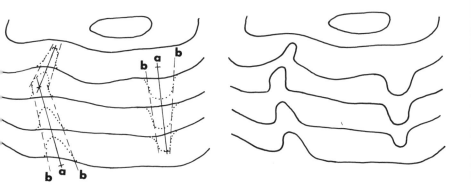

*Drawing in re-entrants.* Drawing in re-entrants and spurs is done by first laying in the center line (a). The width of the feature is then measured and plotted (b). Using the width lines as guides, the new contours are then sketched in.

## Making the Master

### ON PAPER

Using paper for the master map presents several problems. For one, paper is not transparent enough to permit simply tracing the corrections directly on the master as it rests on the map board. Instead, the corrections must be transferred without that aid. And, that's hard to do with accuracy.

In addition, paper copies are normally difficult to erase. White correction fluid (the typist's aid) or scraping with a sharp knife are the best alternatives, though for photographic copies there are liquid eradicators available.

The actual drafting of the corrections must be done in regular drawing ink most of the time (a black ball-point pen is sometimes OK) to give enough contrast.

### ON FILM

With the master on drafting film it's easy to transfer the corrections; the master is simply laid on top of the map board and retraced. If the master is on a clean film, the first step is to draw in several small features to be used as registration marks. The map board is then lined up with the appropriate registration marks before the tracing is begun.

Pencils (drafting-film leads) are easiest to use and may be best for first tries. But it's difficult to control the line width with these pencils and this makes it rather hard to produce a nice looking map. Technical ink pens (tube-tip pens) give perfect results but are expensive and a bit tricky if one is not used to them (see appendix for recommended sizes).

Here are some hints (valid for both tube-tip pen and pencil drafting):

1. *Keep the film clean.* In fact, most of these tips are just amplifications of this basic rule.

2. *Hands should be washed carefully* before work begins.

3. *Use a soft piece of cloth* between the hand and the work as the hand slides over the film.

4. To facilitate the work, *dust the drawing and the cloth piece* with talcum or drafting powder. If the ink doesn't "bite," rub the area with the powdered cloth.

5. *Always be sure the ink is dry* before any area is touched.

6. *Erase with a soft plastic eraser* (drafting-film eraser), with the tip slightly moistened with clean water (not in your mouth!).

## ON WASH-OFF MASTERS

Wash-off masters offer the same advantages as drafting film. In addition, it is not necessary to retrace everything. However, all this is at the cost of a less neat-looking final map, if the master has been enlarged substantially beyond the size of the original.

Perfect erasing of the photo-copied details is easily managed with a lightly-wetted plastic eraser—one of the beauties of the wash-off.

## OVERLAYS

In order to show features that cover larger areas (e.g., marshes, clearings, water bodies and prohibited areas) clearly, it is easiest to use self-adhesive cut-out shading film. These rub-on symbols give very professional looking results and can be applied on film as well as paper. The symbols suggested in the appendix make reference to the brand Letraset, but are also available in other brands, e.g., Mecanoma and Chartpak. Adhesive tapes can be found to show the trails, but they must be of the crepe type to be able to be bent sharply enough.

### ADDING THE LEGEND

Legend and other text may be hand-lettered, typed or rubbed on using transfer lettering, the last giving a superb looking result. For typewritten text, one good method is to type on 3M Magic Mending Tape, or some such matte-finish transparent tape (must be clean), and then tape it on the master. If working with a paper master, the text may be typed directly on the paper or on a separate piece of paper afterwards taped onto the master. Be sure to include complete scale and contour-interval information.

### WORKING IN COLOR

Color maps are produced basically the same way as black and white maps, but separate masters must be drawn for each color. First, the entire *corrected* map is drawn in color pencils on an intermediate master. With this as a base, the separate color masters are then retraced. Registration marks must be included on each master to ensure that the colors can be positioned correctly in relation to each other. For a refresher on legend symbols, see again the appendix and fold-out map.

## Printing (or Reproduction)

The *simplest* and *quickest* way to print maps is to use a regular copying machine. However, the quality achieved using this method is not normally too good and the resulting maps are quite expensive figured per copy. Also, with this method, it is not usually possible to do the reduction "trick" suggested earlier as the best way to obtain really crisp looking copies.

A better way is to offset print, which usually results in very clear and professional-looking copies. The cost will be $10 to $20 for 500 copies. If the map is to be reduced, specify clearly exactly what lesser space on the final printed map a specific distance on the master map is to equal. Or, a percentage figure can be given. (A reduction wheel works well for this if your math is weak.) Instructions—including the reduction information—should be written on the master in light-blue (non-copying) pencil.

Color printing must be done on a press permitting precise registration—which is costly. Heidelberg presses, for one, are recommended. Specify the registration to be less than 5/1,000 of an inch between colors; if any more, the details in two different colors might well change position. For this type of printing, figure on a cost of $150 to $300 for 2,000 8½″ x 11″ copies, or $300 to $500 for 5,000 copies.

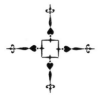

# Meet
# Direction

To ORGANIZE AND RUN an orienteering meet means getting involved in a whole series of activities. But just how much involvement will be required depends mainly on how many participants are expected. At a meet with less than 25 participants one person can handle it all, but to run an event with 500 entries properly a staff of 20 to 30 people is necessary. The accompanying chart spells out the optimum number of helpers needed for meets of various sizes.

However—independent of the size of the meet—one official is always required—the Meet Director. Full responsibility for running the meet will be his (or hers), and he is the one that must have an overall knowledge of the various preparations for the meet and where they stand. At a small event the meet director can do most of the jobs himself, but the bigger the meet, the more jobs should be handed over to other officials. At a major official event, the meet director's most important, and preferably only, job is to see that everyone else does what they are assigned to do. Sometimes, in addition, an assistant meet director is named. He works with the director and should be able to run the event himself should the meet director be prevented from doing so.

One practical precaution valid for everybody with a key job—be prepared for rain. Another must for all is precision; no goofs allowed. Each worker should check and recheck to be sure that his task is done correctly.

## Meet Staff Requirements Guidelines

| FUNCTION | Meet Size | | | |
|---|---|---|---|---|
| | UNDER 25 | UNDER 75 | UNDER 150 | OVER 150 |
| Meet Director | A | A | A | A |
| Course Setter | A | A | A | B |
| Registration | B | B C | B C | C D |
| Start | A | D | D | E F G |
| Finish | A | A | E F | H I J |
| Secretariate | A (B) | A (C) | A (C) | K L (D) |
| Total Staff: | 2 | 4 | 6 | 12 |

( ) indicates that the person has the job at the later part of the meet.

Following is a quick rundown of the chief tasks necessary to the running of a successful meet of local nature, and with a maximum of perhaps 100 participants. Naturally many variations are possible according to each club's taste, but the procedures described here should give all interested in smooth meet organization some good guidelines to follow.

## Meet Director

As we have said, for a small meet one person can manage all or most of these tasks. But, for a meet of this size the meet director will need help. Just how much is a matter of personal choice but for a meet the size we're considering here he would be foolish to consider less than 4. As the chart shows, for a meet of this size, the meet director and course director are one and the same; but he/she would need help at the registration desk and start area and at the secretariat. They would divide the responsibility for the tasks described here pretty much as follows:

### THE PRE-MEET TASKS

1. Find an area suitable for the meet and with adequate parking.

2. Obtain permission for use of the area as necessary, for both the meet and for parking.

The meet director and interested competitor—perhaps checking final meet arrangements. Another important function of the director is to be available for all queries—from seasoned and neophyte competitors alike.

3. Notify the local police of the proposed use of the area and consult them about any parking and traffic problems.

4. Get access to the best available map. If it is not adequate, the meet director will have to plan on a map-maker or, better yet, team, among his job appointees.

5. Recruit an adequate number of helpers to organize and run the meet. Assign tasks and give detailed instructions, as necessary. This includes checking to see how the tasks are proceeding. If map-making or checking is required the map team must be put to work early. As we have seen in the *Map Making* chapter, work with maps takes time.

6. Send preliminary notification about the meet to national and regional orienteering organizations and to neighboring clubs as

Announcing the

# NORTH AMERICAN ORIENTEERING CHAMPIONSHIPS

by The New England Orienteering Club

at Bear Brook State Park, Suncook, New Hampshire

May 24 - 25, 1975

The meet, a two day, total time event, is open to all. However, the title "North American Champion" and the associated awards are reserved for those of one year's residence in the United States or Canada. Beginning orienteers are welcome. A self-guiding instructional trail will be provided both days of the meet.

**EVENTS:**

| Course | Approximate Length of Course | D-Championship Classes | D-Recreational Classes | H-Championship Classes | H-Recreational Classes | Group Class |
|--------|------------------------------|------------------------|------------------------|------------------------|------------------------|-------------|
| Blue | 8-9 km. | | | H21A- | | |
| Red | 5-6 km. | D19A- | | H35A-<br>H19-20A | H (Red) | |
| Orange | 3½-4½ km. | D35A-<br>D15-18A | D (Orange) | H43A-<br>H15-18A | H (Orange) | |
| Yellow | 3½-4½ km. | D-14A | D (Yellow) | H-14A | H (Yellow) | |
| White | 2-3 km. | D (Novice) | | H (Novice) | | H & D Novice |

Classes younger than D19/H21 may step up to higher classes. Classes older than D19/H21 may step down classes, but not more than to D19/H21. (D=Women, H=Men)
Class determined by age reached during 1975.

**ENTRY FEES:**

D19/H19 and up:    $4.00        Non USOF or COF members add $1.00
                   ($2.00 per day)    (White course entries are exempt)

All others:        $2.00
                   ($1.00 per day)

Post entries:   A surcharge of 50%

**REGISTRATION:**

Pre-registration is required in all classes except those competing on the white course. Registration forms must reach NEOC by FRIDAY, MAY 16. All entries received after the above date are considered post-entries. Late registration is possible up to Saturday, May 24 at 11:30 a.m. and will be subject to a 50% surcharge. White course registration will stop at 12 noon on Saturday.

**ENTRY FORM:**

NAME:_____    ENTRY FEE    :_____

ADDRESS:_____    If non-USOF or COF
                                                 member, surcharge
                                                 of $1.00         :_____
        _____
                                                 $0.50 charge for
                                                 results mailed to
CLUB:_____    you personally   :_____

Year of
birth  :_____    Class:_____    TOTAL            :_____

                                                 Make check payable to:
Are you a USOF or COF member?:_____     NEW ENGLAND ORIENTEERING CLU

**WAIVER:**
I hereby release the New England Orienteering Club, the United States Orienteering Federation, their associated clubs, their agents, representatives and members from any and all claims or rights to damages for any injuries or losses incurred by me or my family directly or indirectly during my participation or my family's participation in this Orienteering competition.

Mail entry to:
Jim Plant
50 Glencrest Drive
North Andover, Mass. 01845

Signature _____

If under 18, signature of parent or guardian

# SAMPLE OF A MEET ANNOUNCEMENT AND ENTRY BLANK.

indicated, as soon as the date is firm. The range of the notification would of course hinge somewhat on the size of the meet desired as well as on its aim, size of area, number of helpers, etc.

7. Put together an invitation for the meet giving: type of event, date, times, courses and classes, map information, fees, directions, organizer (including a place or phone number to contact). This invitation of course to be mailed to all members of the host club and to as many other clubs and/or individual orienteers the particular meet warrants; normally, except for the bigger national and semi-national meets, any club within fairly easy driving range might be considered.

8. Publicize the event wherever possible, e.g., to other local outdoor-oriented clubs, to scout troops, at sporting goods stores, in schools, etc. This involves putting together a short news release not only outlining the details of the meet but explaining a bit about orienteering—the release to go to local papers, area magazines and "what's happening" media, along with local radio and TV stations.

9. As the meet approaches check all needed equipment, e.g., control markers, punches, control cards, map cases, rental compasses, master-map boards, pens, felt tip markers, staplers, tape, waiver forms, paper pads, tables, chairs, etc. Most clubs will have most of this equipment already in hand. But it is always necessary to check carefully, so that additional equipment can be purchased, rented or borrowed if necessary—and especially if a larger crowd than usual is expected. Nothing is worse than a meet spoiled by the lack of the right piece of equipment in the right place at the right time, and especially so as this can almost always be avoided by the proverbial ounce of prevention. However, note the alternative equipment suggestions for small beginner meets at the end of this chapter.

10. Check back with the map team to be sure a proper map is in the works and will be ready in time.

11. Check with the course setter to be sure that the preliminary course work has been done properly.

12. Check everything again.

Check List of Equipment and Materials
- [ ] Control Markers
- [ ] Punches
- [ ] Maps
- [ ] Control Description Slips
- [ ] Control Cards (different colors for each course)
- [ ] Book with Waiver Forms
- [ ] Tables (for registration, start, finish)
- [ ] Boards for Master Maps (or extra tables); plastic cases for maps
- [ ] Red Ballpoint Pens (for competitors copying from master maps)
- [ ] Rental Compasses
- [ ] Plastic Map Cases (for sale)
- [ ] List for Recording Rental Compasses (and/or indicated on control card)
- [ ] Pens and Pencils (for registration, timers, etc.)
- [ ] Cashbox (and change to start out with: e.g., $5 in singles and $5 in quarters)
- [ ] Timing Clocks and/or Watches (start table, finish table, plus extra)
- [ ] Form for Recording Start Times (self-made)
- [ ] Form for Recording Finish Times (self-made)
- [ ] Plastic Holders to Display Order of Finish (with stubs of control cards)
- [ ] Notice Board (announcements, news, membership forms, etc.)
- [ ] Stapler (e.g., some competitors like to staple descriptions to map)
- [ ] Large Refuse Cans
- [ ] First Aid Kit

Other items that come in handy: hammer, nails, thumbtacks, paper, poster board, string, magic markers, extra pens and pencils, scissors, scotch tape, adhesive tape, pocket calculator.

Rainy day needs: rain gear for personnel; plastic bags for materials; shelter: canopies and/or tents for registration, map copying, starter, and finish table; master maps should be placed in plastic map cases.

Warm and humid days: water or other liquids for contestants placed at a control on the course and/or at the finish.

## AT THE MEET

As we have said, at a small meet the meet director would have to do most of this himself, but for our purposes, his chief task at the meet is to be sure all areas—final course setting, assembly area coordination, beginners instruction, the start, registration, the finish, time keeping and results, first aid, etc.—we'll learn more about the details of these various jobs as we go on—are running smoothly.

Beyond this, perhaps one of the most important tasks of the meet director is to be sure that when the participants are dispatched they understand they must be sure to return their control card, or sign out, before leaving the meet area, and that they must be sure to return before the maximum time-limit expires.

### AFTER THE MEET

Sometimes it seems there are even more jobs to be done after a meet than before, but once again it is the meet director's responsibility to be sure to either perform the following after-meet chores or to be sure that they are attended to—either right after the meet or as soon after as possible.

1. Clean up and restore the area to its pre-meet condition. An area left neater than found is a certain welcome back.

2. Verify that all controls have been retrieved.

3. Check to be absolutely sure that all the participants have checked out at the finish point before the officials leave the area.

4. If necessary, be prepared to organize search parties to look for anyone still out on the course (check at their home phone first, if possible).

4. Telephone abbreviated results to the news media.

5. Compile the official results to be sent to the newsletter editors of the participating clubs and to the various umbrella organizations.

6. As soon as possible after the meet, send letters of thanks to the land managers, sponsors and other supporters.

## Map Maker

We have already had a good look at what the map-maker does in the chapter of the same name—to either prepare a new map or update an existing one as needed to make it as accurate and fair as possible.

Beyond this, the map-maker is responsible for obtaining an adequate supply of maps for all participants.

## Course Setter

Another very important job—to be checked and counter-checked as often as possible. The meet director will want to give this a close look too. The following is a quick checklist for course setters.

1. Following the instructions in the *Course Setting* chapter, set the needed courses and mark the control locations.

2. Write and print the control descriptions. Care must be taken that these be *precise*.

3. Draw ample master maps. Again, be *precise*. A good rule of thumb: make as many master maps as there are starts per 10-minute period on the course; e.g., if competitors are started every other minute then five master maps are needed.

*Note:* If preparing for a small meet (less than 30 people), it's reasonable to give the participants maps premarked with the course. They are probably chiefly beginners anyhow and just the ones who need this service the most. If possible, *always* give beginners premarked maps to spare them from making course-plotting mistakes. In this event, the master-map task can be eliminated.

4. If needed, mark any necessary map corrections on a number of maps to be posted as map-correction masters.

5. Hang out the control markers the morning of the meet. Controls that are unlikely to be disturbed or vandalized may be hung the day prior to the meet—but check them regardless just before the meet, if possible.

6. Make up the punch masters for each course. These are the cards that let the scorers know which control point carries which punch mark. All qualifying competitors must show cards carrying the right punch in the right spot.

This punching business can sometimes cause problems for the course setter. At courses that cross themselves (e.g., figure-8 shaped) it's very tempting for the runners to take the controls out of order. This can be prevented by having special punching instructions (NEOC multi-punching) at one control at the furtherest part of the loop. The special instructions require the participants to punch the appropriate box—plus the next one, two, or three boxes (varies); then to punch the subsequent controls in the next free

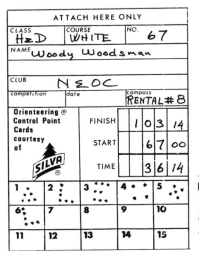

A punched control card. This is the portion of the card that our orienteer, "Woody," carried with him; it is the punches in the boxes at the bottom that must match the master punch card the course setters have made up for his (the White) course.

boxes, maintaining the offset that the multi-punching generated. If the participant tried to take a short cut, he will find himself in quite a mess. However, be sure to announce before the meet start that special multi-punching is to be used on the course—and explaining how it works to any who might not have encountered it before.

7. If the weather is very hot or dry, it's a good service to arrange a water stop on the longer courses.

8. After the meet, take down all controls—after the maximum time for all contestants has expired. Volunteers can be asked to do this, or at least to help.


## Assembly Area Coordinator

The job of the assembly area coordinator is an important one too. Successful completion of these duties—as outlined below— smoothes the coming and going for all and does as much as anything to make the newcomer welcome and to let the old-timer enjoy a superior meet. At smaller meets this job is usually absorbed by the meet director.

1. Set out direction signs to the meet from the nearest major roads all the way in to the parking area; oversee (with helpers) the parking.

2. Put up signs and streamers directing participants from the parking area to the registration and assembly area.

3. Post signs and hang streamers directing attention to the important points of the meet, e.g., registration, start, finish, instructional course, toilets, etc. Also—in an especially obvious spot—have a sign advising rank beginners what to do, i.e., to first go and register. These signs may all be concentrated in one place—an information pole serves this purpose nicely, or perhaps a handy and visible tree.

4. Hang up a model control to show a marker, punch and the code letters.

5. Make the meet area inviting and a bit festive, maybe through a "welcome" banner and some flags.

6. Organize an area where the results will be posted. Make sure that everyone knows where it is.

7. Remove all signs and streamers at the end of the meet.

## Beginner Instruction

This isn't so much a single person's job as it is a matter of club policy. Nonetheless one or more people can be assigned to make sure that the agreed-upon type of beginner instruction is made available at whichever meets seem appropriate—usually a meet at which 10 to 20, or more, rank beginners are expected. At these meets some means to teach basic orienteering facts should be provided.

The next chapter on *Spreading the Word* offers some ideas in its section on common teaching methods. A popular one is the use of a specially prepared self-instruction course (or "self-guiding trail"). Other methods include use of instructors in varying degrees—from the rather rigorous run of a mock meet under careful supervision (or "guided tour") to a more casual "map walk," with the instructor simply explaining the more important fundamentals and pointing out possible pitfalls.

By-standing orienteers can also be of help on the day of the meet by offering help when it's needed.

## Registration

The registration desk is normally the first stopping point for a participant. At the registration area information signs should be posted showing: that it indeed is the registration area, the specific courses to be run and course lengths, maximum times, entry fees, rental compass fee and deposit, prices of items for sale (map cases, extra maps, compasses, etc.), walking time to start. Hanging the signs from a string above the registration table makes them very easy to see.

Most of the above information can also be included in an information handout together with other orienteering news. This

*The registration area.* The line drawing below gives a good idea of the essential organizational bases to be touched at the small- to average-sized meet and lays out a workable activity-flow scheme. It is important that all information so necessary to beginners especially is readily available in a prominent spot. Note, too, that the master-map area allows ample room for copying. As for most smaller meets, the last control leads the finishers back to the same Start/Finish area. This is not only convenient for everyone but permits a small staff to function more efficiently.

information sheet may be given out at the registration desk, or better, at the parking area.

The registration desk can be manned by a single worker but, at a big meet, several work much better.

## REGISTRATION TASKS

1. Give out all necessary event information.

2. Have participants sign a waiver (a slip of paper—pretyped—excusing the meet and its organizers from any damages) and also include their home phone number—good to have if you want to reach them after the meet.

3. Find out what course the participant wants to—or maybe should—enter. Some small groups and families will participate as a single entry. They receive a single card.

4. Fill in the course on a control card, both on the card itself and on the stub (or get a card of appropriate color).

5. Assign and fill in (again on both the card and stub) a start time far enough ahead to include adequate walking time to the start. At the same time, record this time on a time sheet for the course—this to help in keeping a suitable spacing between the participants.

The time is assigned in round minutes only after the first start (O-time). This makes the final time calculations much simpler and safer.

*Note:* This method of assigning starting time at registration allows the competitors to have to watch for their starting time just at the start area. Another way is to assign start time at the start area itself. But this method forces people to stand in line at the start area as well as at the registration desk. This seems an unnecessary nuisance, though with smaller meets it doesn't matter too much.

6. Have the participant fill in his or her name both on the control card and its stub.

7. Give the participant the card, a map and a control description slip. To have the rule that one entry consists of one card and one map makes things simpler. Sell extra maps.

8. Collect the entry fee.

9. Ask the participant to proceed to the start unless they need to buy a map case or rent a compass.

10. Supply any needed equipment: compasses, map cases, extra maps, etc.

11. Have recruiting material for the club and mailing list sign-up sheets available.

12. At the end of the meet task: give back deposits at the return of rental compasses.

13. Be prepared for rain! Plastic sheeting or a tarp can be used as a rain tent over the registration area.

14. A big job!

## The Start

At least one worker will be needed to supervise the *start* area. More would be better.

The start described below uses the master-map system, with start times assigned at registration.

### PRELIMINARIES

1. Tape the master maps (in waterproof cases) on tables or hard-surface boards (door skin or paneling plywood is light weight and works well). Allow enough room so that the master map and two participants' maps will fit on the board without obscuring each other (12" x 25" is good). Attach good-quality, red ballpoint pens to the boards with firmly attached strings.

2. Keep master maps for each course separated, with course signs clearly displayed above them. Label each master map also.

3. Be prepared for rain. Tie plastic tarps above the master maps if it rains. It's impossible to draw accurate courses on wet maps!

### DURING THE START

1. Hold all waiting starters behind a waiting line.

2. Collect the responding participants' stubs (check first that it is indeed their turn). Let them advance to the Start line after having made them aware of where their master maps are.

Note: If premarked maps are used, they can be given out when the stubs are collected.

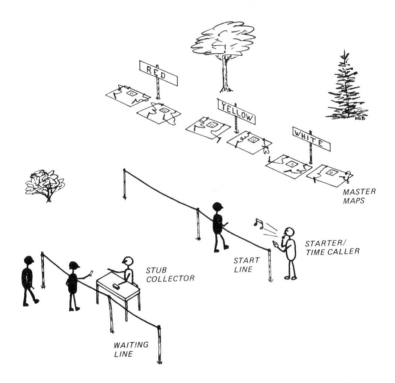

The start area. A larger meet requires a separate start area. Here, one worker collects the already filled-in control card stubs for later transmission to the results keepers, while another worker acts as starter and time caller, directing the orienteers to the master-map area and on to the course at the appropriate time. It is essential that this operation run smoothly—no easy task at a large meet—as, to be fair, the actual start time and the time noted on the competitor's stub must be one and the same. Beyond that, even with a start every minute, it takes a good while to get a large group out on the course.

Here the starter is noting a competitor's start time. Later he will have to forward this information on the competitor's control card stub to the secretariat where the lapsed time will be figured.

3. Send the starters to the master maps at the sound of the start. To sound the start use a motorcycle horn or loud whistle.

4. Call the next start time as soon as the previous start time is up —a new start every minute.

5. Send the stubs to the secretariat now and then. Don't lose them. They are the records of the people out on the course!

Note: Assigning start times could have been done when picking the next starter from the waiting line.

LAST
CONTROL

*The finish area.* Whenever possible for a larger meet it's nice to have a finish "chute" and separate desk. This allows the workers to concentrate on their job—recording the finishers' time and posting the results (on a nearby board) as quickly as possible. However, for everyone's convenience—as with the smaller meet—this area should ideally be situated close to the start and parking areas.

## The Finish

Here again several workers will make lighter work of a very demanding task.

### BEFORE THE FIRST START

1. Designate and organize the finish area so the incoming runners can only approach the finish from one direction and so they can be seen at a good distance.

2. Construct a finish "chute" with a finish banner displayed above it if the size of the field merits this. For most meets, a simple corral set off with some streamered lines and a finish sign or two should do it.

3. Coordinate the finish clock with the starters. To do this first decide upon an *O-time* when all timing clocks should show an exact hour, e.g., 10 o'clock. Make some auxiliary faces to fit around the clock to make it easier to read the minutes only. Graduate one face 60–120; another 120–180, etc., in 60-minute intervals.

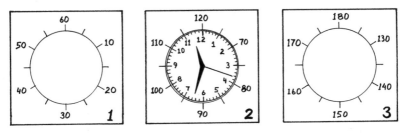

*The finish clock.* Exchangeable auxiliary faces fitting around the finish clock make it easier to read time in minutes from O-time. The actual time in number 2 above shows 92:18. O-time was 10 o'clock.

TIMING THE FINISHERS

1. The timer reads the finish clock and records the time for each participant by number in order on a slip of paper every time a runner crosses the finish line.

2. At the same time, the control-card collector retrieves the cards from the runners in the order they came in. It's important to keep this straight! If at any time a finisher crosses the finish line without a control card insert a blank card as a substitute. This is especially important at busy times to keep things straight.

3. At breaks, tear off the time slip and clip it together with the appropriate collected control cards with a strong, large paper clip.

4. Transfer the recorded times from the slips to the control cards at convenient times as soon as possible.

5. Mark cards from participants that did not complete the course with DNF (did not fulfill).

6. Send the completed cards to the secretariat.

## Secretariat (Results Keeper)

It's advisable to have this job (desk) set up in a protected area away from wind, rain and curious orienteers. Once again the necessary number of workers varies with the size of the meet but more workers will certainly allow this crucial time to go more smoothly. The secretariat's chores are as follows.

Here a competitor makes his last spurt to the finish through the finish chute. Most club meets would offer the simpler finish area shown in the earlier drawing.

1. Check the punch marks on the incoming cards against the punch masters. According to the rules a runner should be disqualified if: *the card shows an incorrect punch; all required punches are not shown; the punches are out of order.* Mark any disqualified cards with DSQ.

Note: In the case of illegible punches some flexibility is good, especially in the case of younger runners.

2. Calculate the times on the good cards. And then—check the calculation *a second time* for good measure.

3. Find the stubs for the calculated cards by matching the courses run and start times. Transfer the results to the stubs.

4. Post the result on the result board using the now-completed stub; e.g., in a plastic result frame.

Note: Tab is kept on participants remaining out on the courses by checking against the number of unmatched stubs left.

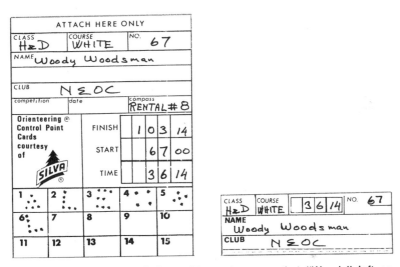

*A completed control card.* From this card we see that "Woody" left on the White course 67 minutes after 0-time. If 0-time was 10 a.m., he actually started at 11:07:00. His start time was also used as his start number (67). At the finish, his card was checked carefully to be sure the correct punch marks appeared in the proper boxes according to the master punch card for his course—let's say they did. His finish time—36 minutes and 14 seconds—was then recorded, both on his own card and on the stub he left behind at the start—let's say it was good.

## First Aid

Always have some type of first aid available. At smaller meets access to a good first aid kit might suffice, but at a major event it's a good idea to affiliate with some group that has first aid as part of its program.

## Beginner's Meet Equipment

In our discussion of meet organization we have called for use of considerable equipment that few starting groups would have access to—e.g., control markers, punches, result frames, etc. But that is no reason to prevent an interested orienteer from organizing and run-

*The results.* A staff member posting the final results—always an eagerly awaited moment.

ning a meet. These missing pieces of equipment can easily be worked around or substituted for.

Here are some suggestions—but let your imagination go to work as well:

Instead of control markers you can use cardboard boxes or empty plastic gallon bottles painted orange (red) and white. Wide plastic or fabric ribbons will also do, as will big milk cartons, especially if the side corners are cut open.

Punches can be substituted for by using a system under which different colored pencils (waterproof!) or crayons are hung at the controls. The runners check off the appropriate control box with the various pencils, giving each box a unique color code.

Another way is to have a special check code on the marker in addition to the control code. The runners must then copy that check code over to the correct box on the control card using a pencil hanging from the marker. Put that check code at the lower part of the marker and draw a circle around it to avoid confusion with the code letter.

In fact, control cards may even be done away with by including punch boxes on the map, or better, on the control description sheet.

As to results: they don't have to be posted at all if less then 20 or so people participate. They can be checked directly from a list giving the finish times or from the collected cards. Results may also be posted using thumbtacks on a soft board allowing easy rearranging. If a curved (convex) board is used, the result stubs can be held down by sticking them under an elastic band running along the curvature.

Compasses might be more of a problem. However, it is usually possible to find a couple of rental compasses, and/or scrounge a few from among friends or from a local scout troop.

*Award time.* A fun time—though awards at all but the most advanced orienteering meets are kept very simple.

## A Sanctioned Meet

The organization for a COF/USOF (the Canadian and U.S. Orienteering federations) sanctioned meet has basically the same structure as the local meet outlined above, but is naturally bigger. For such a meet, *nothing* is allowed to go wrong; a solid organization with enough helpers is the base for a perfect meet. Sanctioning dictates specific requirements in several of the areas—for example map standardization, set classes and courses, course setting, etc.

These requirements, together with the size of the meet, normally necessitate several new club functions, such as mailing wide-ranging invitations, a meet secretary, meet treasurer, pre-registration venture stand (for selling T-shirts, etc.), refreshment stand, jury, awards, awards presentation, etc.

At small local meets awards are not necessary. But at a major meet the three top finishers in each class should receive awards (more only becomes too much icing on the cake).

Experience is the best teacher of course so try to make it to a large sanctioned meet now and then—you should be able to pick up some very useful organizational pointers there.

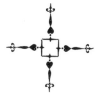

# Spreading
# The Word

ORIENTEERING'S APPEAL to many different kinds of people is truly amazing. Accordingly, participation in orienteering as a sport has grown in leaps and bounds around the world wherever a small seed of interest is planted. Take one enthusiastic orienteer, place him wherever orienteering has not caught on, and given a few years, a group of gung-ho orienteers will follow.

The advantages of encouraging other orienteers in an area are obvious. The meets can be larger, more frequent, more varied—and more sociable. For, as we have said before, orienteering contains a large social factor. In addition to the opportunity to rehash each meet with others—something all orienteers seem to relish—it's just more fun to orienteer in company.

Competition is another factor. There can be a little bit, or a lot —depending on the individual—in all of us; sometimes we just want to know how we stack up against our peers alone in the woods with a map and compass and working against time. Running in meets gives all this opportunity if they want it.

Some orienteers are not the slightest interested in competition and that brings us to even another reason for finding additional fellow orienteers: with larger groups of people there can be a greater sharing of the work load. Nobody wants to be the *only* meet organizer. It takes work but there are many advantages to encouraging others to try the sport.

## The Club

From our experience, and from the past history in Canada and Europe, the club is the best vehicle to spread orienteering's word. Traditionally, the pockets of enthusiastic orienteers in Europe and North America are centered around a core of enthusiastic individual orienteers who have formed local orienteering clubs.

You don't have to be an expert to be the catalyst to get a club started. Every movement needs an instigator—enthusiasm *alone* can go a long way when it comes to introducing others to orienteering. Perhaps you already have friends from other outdoor activities who might be prime candidates for a fledgling orienteering group. Do you canoe, hike, or ski with others during the year? Perhaps your fellow participants in those activities will be interested.

Follow (adapting as necessary for a small meet) the guidelines given in the previous chapter and put on a meet of your own to get things started. It won't take very many of you. The first couple of meets will be the hardest to get organized—but, with some advance planning, you can run a successful meet. Put an article in the local paper to draw people from beyond your immediate circle of friends. We in our area have had great cooperation from local newspapers. Don't be afraid to try or to ask others for their help. It works.

Why have a club? . . .

## CLUB FUNCTIONS

There are three major functions of an orienteering club; though, in fact, some clubs go beyond simple orienteering and dabble in skiing or social events. But let's look here at the ones that stick pretty closely to orienteering.

*Running Meets.* This is the first function of any orienteering club. It may sound simple, but if orienteering is to grow, running successful meets must be any club's major effort. Meet schedules must be planned ahead. Meet organizers must be found (lots of encouragement is sometimes required here). Promising new areas for future meets must be explored and maps prepared, etc., etc. And it all takes people.

*Promoting Interest.* This goes hand in hand with running meets, of course, but should be any club's *second* serious concern. Once the sport catches on in an area, this task is not so difficult, but it's not so easy at first.

Publicity will play a big role in a new club's success. From our own experience we have found that one of the best tools for spreading the word is the club *newsletter.* A simply prepared brochure filled with orienteering news can arouse a lot of interest. Items on upcoming events and meet results, and general orienteering news in both North America and Europe—plus perhaps a local "Personals" column—could be included. Not only does a newsletter serve to interest beginners, it also serves as a cohesive bond for the club as a whole. Often many miles separate club members and a periodic newsletter does a lot to bridge this distance—and keep interest alive.

There are other good sources of publicity. Local newspapers, as we've said before, are an excellent means through which to publicize upcoming meets. And why not send the same editor a copy of the meet results? Radio stations are required to allow time for items of community interest. Find out in what form they want information on orienteering and send it in. During the days of orien-

*Club promotion.* The use of special awards and offering handmade mementos for sale are ways to help build club interest—and fun too. These are examples used by the New England Orienteering Club (NEOC).

teering's infancy in the Boston area, we were lucky enough to get a brief twelve-minute shot on a television show about all the different ways one could spend leisure time in Boston. Wham! The next week we had over 100 participants at a local event—more than double the previous attendance.

*As Resource Center.* The third function of an orienteering club is to act as a resource center for others in the community. There are no doubt many groups in your area whose activities border on the periphery of orienteering—college outing clubs, Boy Scouts, YMCA's, Rod and Gun clubs, ski patrols and clubs, and various church and school youth groups will all have members who would be interested to learn what orienteering is all about. They may not all want to become competitive orienteers, but your club can certainly add a lot to their programs by teaching *those interested* how to orienteer. And who knows, you may get some new club members in the process!

## CLUB STRUCTURE

Orienteering clubs can be put together in any way that is comfortable and works for its members, but our club (NEOC) has found that a few specific jobs have to be done if the club is to meet the three functions just described. Each of these positions exists for a purpose, not just to create an empty chair. In our club these continuing jobs are tended to by either the club officers or committee chairmen, as follows:

*The President.* The President, or "El Presidente," is responsible for the overall club operation and supervises the other club officers. (Just to keep the record straight, our club's birth took place upstairs in a Cambridge bar, late one March night in 1972. Due to the circumstances of the evening, nobody can remember for sure exactly how many were there or the names of all those present, but there were at least six of us. Hopefully, your club had, or will have, a more orderly beginning.) The president has also served as the primary recruiter of club personnel. He is elected yearly at an annual club meeting, as are the other officers.

*The Secretary.* In NEOC, the secretary is in charge of the entire communication area—correspondence, proposals for new map areas, and club announcements fall under his, or her, jurisdiction. In a small club, the secretary can also handle the newsletter operations.

*The Treasurer.* Keeping the financial picture straight is the task of any club treasurer; in our club he has the added responsibility of keeping track of the membership rolls. The treasurer receives all membership fees (in NEOC, $3.00 a year), handles and accounts for all the meet expenses and receipts, and keeps an up-to-date membership list, complete with full address and phone number.

*Map-making Officer.* This is the member chiefly responsible for searching out areas suitable for new map-making projects, and once found, for developing such maps.

Good maps of good areas are the lifeblood of orienteering. If a club uses only a limited number of areas for its meets, the members will soon become too familiar with their features—relying more on memory than on navigation skills. The events soon become lack-lustre. To avoid such stagnation, new parks and other areas must be found constantly. As we have seen in the *Map Making* chapter, preparing new orienteering maps can be an enormous task, so much of the success of any orienteering club rests on the shoulders of its map-making officer.

*Meet Scheduling Chairman.* Some clubs refer to this job as Competition Committee Chairman, but no matter its title, the job is one and the same. Orienteering meets must be planned well in advance to ensure adequate publicity and proper spacing between meets. National orienteering federations require advance information on important meets for sanctioning purposes. These considerations are the bailiwick of the meet scheduling chairman.

*Newsletter Editor and Distributor.* The newsletter is a big job, and though some clubs may delegate this responsibility to just one member, our club places two people on the job. One person serves as the editor, gathering meet results, schedules and general news. Another member, who preferably owns or has access to a mimeograph machine, handles the printing and mailing aspect. At first, when the secretary (one of the authors) handled the job, the newsletter appeared only sporadically; now, with a better system, the NEOC newsletter is a quarterly journal.

*Publicity Director.* This is another position which can make or break a club. Sports editors with a willing ear must be found and fed full information on the virtues of orienteering. Newspaper deadlines must be met to ensure publication of event notices and results. Speakers from the club must be recruited to speak to various community groups, etc. The publicity director has a big hand in the success and growth of the club.

Other official positions may well be required as a club grows. In the near future our own club may need an equipment manager. With two or three meets a month in the spring and fall, our club's equipment gets quite a workout. Many times we wonder, "who has how many rental compasses?" or "who had all the control markers and punches last?" Life would be a good bit easier with one club member responsible for keeping track of the equipment and acting as a dispatcher.

Another official our club may soon need is an education director. Because of recent publicity we are continually being asked to provide speakers at conventions, clinics, and various schools. An education director could develop a teaching packet (more on that later) and be responsible to line up various club members to fill the speaker requests as they are received.

These are just two positions that our club may need to fill soon. Perhaps there will be others as we continue to grow. Another club —including our own—might have different priorities as it grows. But, as a club we are thankful that we need all these jobs done, and that there are so many hands to pitch in when needed.

## Teaching Others

As we have seen, one of the jobs of the members of an orienteering club is to share their knowledge of the sport with others. This can be done both on and off the event course. The following will give anyone called upon to serve this function some ideas as to how to go about it.

### SOME GROUND RULES

Before you get fired up to go out and teach orienteering to others, take some time to learn the skills yourself. Enthusiasm goes a long way in trying to sell something, but you must have knowledge to go with it. Practice the techniques of orienteering shown earlier in the book to the point that you feel comfortable with them. It is not necessary to be a world-class orienteer to teach

Some say that the post-meet post mortems are the best part of all.

the game, but it is necessary to be familiar with the basics. The following is a good list of do's and don'ts for those working to teach others about orienteering. They tell a lot about how the learning takes place.

1. *Orienteering is learned by doing*, not listening. People learn how to read maps and operate compasses by experience. Books and instructional manuals can be of great help, as can the encouragement of others, but the best learning tool is to get out and do. So take any group you work with outside to try their hand at an actual orienteering exercise as soon as possible. There are some teaching situations which require, and even benefit from, hours in the classroom, but a lecture format restricts the learning process when it comes to orienteering.

2. When presenting the fundamental techniques, follow the order given in the *Map and Compass* chapter. Beginners should not have

to rely on their compasses during their first orienteering experience. The map is the Number One item for the beginning orienteer.

3. The novice's first lesson must be at a very simple level to ensure success. Place the controls at obvious locations to allow all the beginners to find them. If the novice has a positive experience on his first outing, chances are he, or she, will be hooked. The teacher should do anything possible to provide that experience. *An instructional course cannot be too easy.* There will always be more difficult courses in the future, but failure on the initial try may keep the newcomer from ever reaching them—by default. Study the White course on the fold-out map.

4. In keeping with rule #3, *make the lesson fun!* Orienteering is a game—not an army survival drill. Challenge beginners to try their skill—and luck. Then get to the course. If you can stimulate excitement among the participants, questions and thus learning will result. Use whatever imagination and creativity you can muster to bring out the spirit of play that lurks somewhere in everyone. Some of the exercises given in the *Training* chapter should help in this.

## COMMON TEACHING METHODS

Remembering the ground rules above, try one of these common methods for teaching orienteering.

1. *The Direct Method.* Under this method, every effort is made to provide a close replica of an official meet. There is a Start area, the participants are timed and must locate all the controls. Obviously, some brief instruction as to the various elements encountered in an orienteering meet must be given before the start, but the operating idea is that the novice (or "wayfarer") is to be led through a "meet" as his first lesson. For this method to work, there must be several instructors—not only at the assembly, start and finish areas but also along the course. Once the beginner is on the course, the instructors should provide help only when needed. Some beginners will breeze through the very elementary course set, others will require more guidance, but all will get the feeling of orienteering and the satisfaction of completing the course.

2. *The Guided Tour.* This is a modification of method #1 that

has proven quite successful with some instructors. Once again, a beginner's course is set but the meet-like aspects of the start and finish are dropped. The beginners are divided up, with at least one instructor per group. The instructor then presents the bare essentials of the game to his group and guides them along the course, adding further instructions as the course demands them. This method allows less room for individual ability but works well with relatively few instructors.

3. *Self-Guiding Trail.* What can you do if you are all by yourself instructing a group? No problem—in fact, in a pinch this method —once set up—can work without any instructor at all. Imitating the self-guiding nature trail which state and national parks are now offering in some areas, why not a self-guiding orienteering trail?

To create such a course simply lay out a 1-Km- to 1-mile-long trail, with surveyors tape or streamers showing the route. Run the course along interesting features and place numbers at the prominent ones. At the beginning of the trail, the beginners are given a map and an information sheet explaining what the features at the corresponding numbers are.

> · *Example:* No. 1—A knoll. A knoll is a small hill which is shown on the map as ⬭ . Each ring stands for a ten-foot change in elevation. Can you see any other knolls from where you are now?

As he, or she, works his way around the trail, the beginner learns to see where he is and what various features look like on the map. By the end of the trail, not only has the budding orienteer had a good walk, he has learned the basic map features and a little bit about how to use a compass. Not all learn equally well under this self-motivating method but it is a good string to have to your bow in your efforts to share your knowledge of, and enthusiasm for, orienteering with newcomers. And many times it is advantageous to have such a trail available at regular orienteering meets to give the "wayfarers" a little preliminary assistance.

Very likely your club will develop its own methods for working with the newcomers that come its way. Any method is fine as long as it works and helps to build interest in the fine sport of orienteering.

# Orienteering
# Clubs

*U.S. ORIENTEERING CLUBS*
*(in alphabetical order by club name)*

National U.S.O.F. office:
United States Orienteering Federation
P.O. Box 500
Athens, Ohio   45701

A & I OC
AROTC, Texas A & I Univ.
Kingsville, TX   78363

Bayou Raiders
c/o Cpt. Joseph Cancellare
Dept. of Mil. Sci., NLU
Monroe, LA   71201

Cambridge Sports Union
c/o Lawrence Berman
23 Fayette St.
Cambridge, MA   02139

Central Michigan OC
5th USROTC Instr. Gp., CMU
Mount Pleasant, MI   48858

Central Ohio OC
c/o David Pintar
2148 Pine Ridge Road
Wickliffe, OH   44092

Chicago Area OC
c/o Michael Connolly
2136 Lake Avenue
Wilmette, IL   60091

Cleveland CC
24451 Lakeshore Blvd., #313 W
Euclid, OH   44123

Delaware Valley OC
c/o Caroline Ringo
212 Westover Drive
Cherry Hill, NJ   08034

Eastman Kodak OC
c/o Robert Phillips
59 Brentwood Drive
Penfield, NY   14526

Flatland OC
c/o John F. Organek
Univ. of Illinois
Champaign, IL   61820

Florida State Univ. OC
USAROTC Instr. Gp., FSU
Tallahassee, FL   32306

Furman OC
AROTC Instr. Gp., FU
Greenville, SC   29613

Gonzaga Univ/ROTC OC
c/o Mil. Sci. Department
Gonzaga University
East 502 Boone Ave.
Spokane, WA   99258

Grazoo OC
c/o Al van Staveren
Goldsworth Valley Apt. R1
Kalamazoo, MI   49008

Griffin OC
c/o AFKA-GCE-GC
P.O. Box 9307
Charlotte, NC   28299

Indiana Univ. of PA OC
c/o Maj. Winston Clark
Dept. of Mil. Sci., IUP
Indiana, PA   15701

Kansas State Univ. OC
c/o Frank Vovk
1709 Ranser Road
Manhattan, KS   66502

Lake Superior State College OC
ROTC Dept., LSSC
Sault Ste. Marie, MI   49783

LaPorte OC
c/o George Harris
113 Grand Ave.
LaPorte, IN   46350

Maryland National Guard OC
121st Engr. Bn, State Armory
Ellicott City, MD   21043

Minnesota OC
c/o Wm. R. Schmidt
Rt. #3 Box 298 A
Faribault, MN   55021

New England OC
c/o Hans Bengtsson
Garrison House Lane
Sudbury, MA   01776

Northern Michigan Univ. OC
Dept. of Mil. Sci., NMU
Marquette, MI   49855

OC of Alfred
P.O. Box 34
Alfred Station, NY   14803

OCONEE OC
c/o Bill Cheatum
100 Torrey Pine Place
Athens, GA   30601

Old Dominican Univ. OC
Dept. of Mil. Sci., ODU
Norfolk, VA   23508

Orange County OC
c/o Thomas Wilson
14362 Willowlane
Westminster, CA   92683

Pathfinder OC
USAROTC Instr Gp
Carnegie Melon Univ.
Pittsburgh, PA   15213

Possum Trot OC
P.O. Box 196
Grandview, MO   64030

Quantico OC
P.O. Box 99
Quantico, VA   22134

Ramapo OC
c/o Larry Crane
157 Lincoln Ave.
Ridgewood, NJ   07450

Rochester OC
c/o Robert F. Phillips
59 Brentwood Drive
Penfield, NY   14526

Rocky Mountain OC
c/o Roger Schoenstein
2618 Meade Circle
Colorado Springs, CO   80907

San Diego OC
c/o Gail Hanna
4076 Crown Point Rd.
San Diego, CA   92109

Southeast Ohio OC
c/o John Cornwell
P.O. Box 1081
Athens, OH   45701

Southern Illinois OC
c/o Kenneth Ackerman
RR #3
Carbondale, IL   62901

St. Bonaventure Raiders
Dept. of Mil. Sci., SBU
St. Bonaventure, NY   14778

St.Louis OC
Box 1206 Washington U
St. Louis, MO    63130

Trojan OC
c/o Carole Shoptaw
1735 Swann St.
Fayetteville, NC    28303

Univ. of Dayton OC
Dept. of Mil. Sci., UD
Dayton, OH    45469

Univ. of Idaho OC
Dept. of Mil. Sci., UI
Moscow, ID    83483

Univ. of New Hampshire OC
c/o Robert Bilodeau
305 Upper 6th St.
Dover, NH    03820

U of Richmond OC
c/o USAROTC
U of Richmond
Richmond, VA    23173

Upper Cumberland OC
Tennessee Tech. Univ., Box 5067
Cookeville, TN    38501

USMA OC
c/o Bud Fish
3028 B Stoney Lonesome
West Point, NY    10996

USSA-CD Examiners Committee
c/o Wesley Doak
Box 529, Indian Lake Resort
Woodruff, WI    54568

Westchester OC
L S Walsh
25 Griffen Ave
Bedford Hills, NY    10507

Western Kentucky U OC
USAROTC Instr Gp
Bowling Green, KY    42101

## CANADIAN ORIENTEERING ASSOCIATIONS
(alphabetically by province)

National C.O.F. office:
Canadian   Orienteering   Federation
333 River Street
Vanier City, Ottawa, Ontario

Alberta Orienteering Association
c/o Mr. Orson Gadowsky
11614–75th Ave.
Edmonton, Alberta

Orienteering Association of B.C.
c/o Prof. A. Anthony
University of B.C. Faculty of Ed.
Vancouver, B.C. V6T 1W5

Manitoba   Orienteering   Association
c/o Mr. Jack Forsyth
Box 163
Hartney, Manitoba

Orienteering Association of N.B.
c/o Mr. Andy Martin
University of N.B. Faculty of Ed.
Fredericton, N.B.

Newfoundland Orienteering Association
c/o Mr. Arthur Robinson
22 Blackwood Place
St. John's, Nfld. ALB 2K6

N.W.T. Orienteering Association
c/o Mr. Jack VanPelt
Box 687
Fort Smith, N.W.T.

Orienteering Association of N.S.
6260 Quinpool Road
Halifax, Nova Scotia B3L 1A3

Ontario Orienteering Association
559 Jarvis Street
Toronto, Ontario

Prince Edward Island Orienteering Association
c/o Mr. Lou Daley
Morell High School
Morell, P.E.I. COA 1SO

Orienteering Quebec
1415 Jarry Street East
Montreal, Quebec H3E 2Z7

Saskatchewan Orienteering Association
c/o Mr. Keith Wilson
907B Argyle Ave.
Saskatoon, Sask. S7H 2V9

Orienteering for the Yukon
c/o Mr. Lawrence Kristalovich
Christ the King Elementary School
Whitehorse, Yukon

*International Orienteering Federation office:*
International Orienteering Federation
c/o Frau Lillvor Silander-Johansson
Huginvägen 2
194 00 Upplands Väsby
Sweden

# Topographic Map
# Symbols

*(Variations will be found on older maps)*

| | |
|---|---|
| Hard surface, heavy-duty road | |
| Hard surface, medium-duty road | |
| Improved light-duty road | |
| Unimproved dirt road | |
| Trail | |
| Railroad: single track | |
| Railroad: multiple track | |
| Bridge | |
| Drawbridge | |
| Tunnel | |
| Footbridge | |
| Overpass—Underpass | |
| Power transmission line with located tower | |
| Landmark line (labeled as to type) | TELEPHONE |
| Dam with lock | |
| Canal with lock | |
| Large dam | |
| Small dam: masonry — earth | |
| Buildings (dwelling, place of employment, etc.) | |
| School—Church—Cemeteries | Cem |
| Buildings (barn, warehouse, etc.) | |
| Tanks; oil, water, etc. (labeled only if water) | Water Tank |
| Wells other than water (labeled as to type) | o Oil ........ o Gas |

| | | |
|---|---|---|
| U.S. mineral or location monument — Prospect | ▲ | x |
| Quarry — Gravel pit | ⊗ | ⋈ |
| Mine shaft—Tunnel or cave entrance | ◾ | Y |
| Campsite — Picnic area | ⅄ | ⊼ |
| Located or landmark object—Windmill | ○ | 𝕏 |
| Exposed wreck | | |
| Rock or coral reef | | |
| Foreshore flat | | |
| Rock: bare or awash | * | ☀ |

| | |
|---|---|
| Horizontal control station | △ |
| Vertical control station | BM ×671 × ×672 |
| Road fork — Section corner with elevation | 429 +58 |
| Checked spot elevation | × 5970 |
| Unchecked spot elevation | × 5970 |

| | |
|---|---|
| Boundary: national | ▬ ▬ ▬ |
| State | ▬ ▬ ▬ |
| county, parish, municipio | ▬ ▬ ▬ |
| civil township, precinct, town, barrio | ▬ ▬ ▬ ▬ |
| incorporated city, village, town, hamlet | ▬ ▬ ▬ ▬ ▬ |
| reservation, national or state | ▬ . ▬ . |
| small park, cemetery, airport, etc. | ▬ ▬ ▬ ▬ ▬ |
| land grant | ▬ . ▬ .. |
| Township or range line, U.S. land survey | ▬▬▬▬ |
| Section line, U.S. land survey | ▬▬▬ |
| Township line, not U.S. land survey | |
| Section line, not U.S. land survey | |
| Fence line or field line | ▬ ▬ ▬ ▬ |
| Section corner: found—indicated | + + |
| Boundary monument: land grant—other | ▫ ▫ |

| | | | |
|---|---|---|---|
| Index contour | | Intermediate contour | |
| Supplementary cont. | | Depression contours | |
| Cut — Fill | | Levee | |
| Mine dump | | Large wash | |
| Dune area | | Tailings pond | |
| Sand area | | Distorted surface | |
| Tailings | | Gravel beach | |
| Glacier | | Intermittent streams | |
| Perennial streams | | Aqueduct tunnel | |
| Water well—Spring | | Falls | |
| Rapids | | Intermittent lake | |
| Channel | | Small wash | |
| Sounding—Depth curve | | Marsh (swamp) | |
| Dry lake bed | | Inundated area | |
| Woodland | | Mangrove | |
| Submerged marsh | | Scrub | |
| Orchard | | Wooded marsh | |
| Vineyard | | Bldg. omission area | |

—From The Department of Interior Geological Survey booklet, *Topographic Maps*, published in April, 1969.

# Symbols for
# Black and White O-Maps

This is only a suggested list of symbols for use on black and white orienteering maps, since no standard set exists for such symbols. The symbols and their dimensions are shown for drafting at 2 times the final printed size. Reduction to half size (or 50%) must be done by the printer before printing.

The list is based on IOF symbols but omissions and modifications have been made to insure clarity and legibility with printing in only black and white. Omissions have also been made to simplify the classification of features. A first-time mapper can with advantage simplify further by ignoring some of the finer classifications and/or more sophisticated symbols; e.g., vegetation symbols, intermediate form contours, ravines/gullies, drainage beds—to mention some.

A minimum of pens (line widths) have been employed—.2, .4 and .8 mm, doubling in size for every new pen (these are the o.—numbers at the left of the symbols). The micronorm series—.18, .35 and .7 mm—will do equally well. If using pens of the various other numbering systems, always check their metric equivalent—the systems vary greatly.

Also, a very basic set of dimensions has been used—all in millimeters. Their approximate equivalents in inches are as follows:

1 mm—⅓ of ⅛ inch
2 mm—⅔ of ⅛ inch
3 mm—⅛ inch
6 mm—¼ inch
12 mm—½ inch

Don't draw any symbols smaller than 1 mm.

To avoid cluttering and illegibility, some space (approximately ½ mm) must be left around small symbols; e.g. as in a contour line if it crosses a small symbol like a boulder. Also, it is wise to leave out less important symbols if features are on top or very close to each other.

Symbols for color maps are described in IOF literature, which should be available from your national office; you will also find a generous sampling on the fold-out map at the back of *Orienteering for Sport and Pleasure*.

## MAN-MADE FEATURES

0.4 ══════ ≈ 1 min.   *Paved Road*
                      *(adjust line width to the*
                      *width of the roadbed)*

0.8 ▬▬▬▬ 0.8 min.   *Unpaved Road*
                     *(adjust line width to the*
                     *width of the roadbed)*

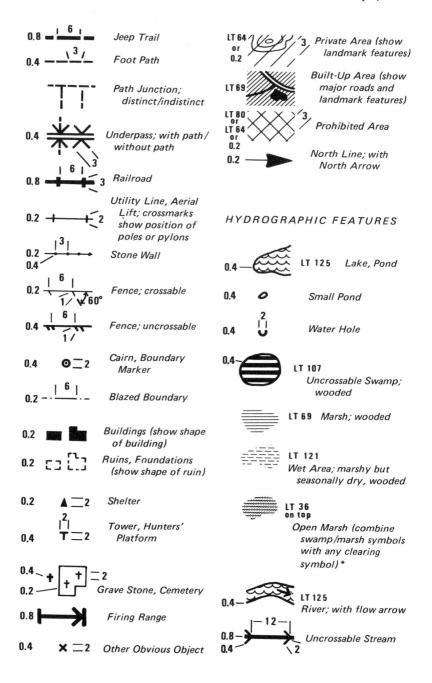

0.8    6    Jeep Trail

0.4    3    Foot Path

Path Junction; distinct/indistinct

0.4    Underpass; with path/ without path

0.8    6    3    Railroad    3

0.2    2    Utility Line, Aerial Lift; crossmarks show position of poles or pylons

0.2
0.4    3    Stone Wall

0.2    6    1/ 60°    Fence; crossable

0.4    6    1/    Fence; uncrossable

0.4    ⊙ ═2    Cairn, Boundary Marker

0.2    6    Blazed Boundary

0.2    Buildings (show shape of building)

0.2    Ruins, Foundations (show shape of ruin)

0.2    ▲ ═2    Shelter

0.4    T ═2    Tower, Hunters' Platform

0.4
0.2    + +    ═2    Grave Stone, Cemetery

0.8    Firing Range

0.4    ✗ ═2    Other Obvious Object

LT 64 or 0.2    3    Private Area (show landmark features)

LT 69    Built-Up Area (show major roads and landmark features)

LT 80 or LT 64 or 0.2    3    Prohibited Area

0.2    North Line; with North Arrow

## HYDROGRAPHIC FEATURES

0.4    LT 125    Lake, Pond

0.4    Small Pond

0.4    2    Water Hole

0.4    LT 107    Uncrossable Swamp; wooded

LT 69    Marsh; wooded

LT 121    Wet Area; marshy but seasonally dry, wooded

LT 36 on top    Open Marsh (combine swamp/marsh symbols with any clearing symbol)*

0.4    LT 125    River; with flow arrow

0.8
0.4    12    2    Uncrossable Stream

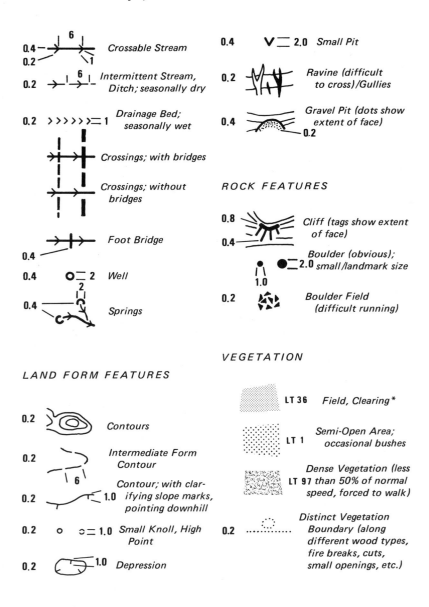

0.4
0.2 — Crossable Stream

0.2 — Intermittent Stream, Ditch; seasonally dry

0.2 — Drainage Bed; seasonally wet

Crossings; with bridges

Crossings; without bridges

Foot Bridge
0.4

0.4 — Well

0.4 — Springs

## LAND FORM FEATURES

0.2 — Contours

0.2 — Intermediate Form Contour

0.2 — Contour; with clarifying slope marks, pointing downhill

0.2 — Small Knoll, High Point

0.2 — Depression

0.4 — V⌐ 2.0 Small Pit

0.2 — Ravine (difficult to cross)/Gullies

0.4 — Gravel Pit (dots show extent of face) 0.2

## ROCK FEATURES

0.8
0.4 — Cliff (tags show extent of face)

Boulder (obvious); small/landmark size
1.0 ●⌐ 2.0

0.2 — Boulder Field (difficult running)

## VEGETATION

LT 36 Field, Clearing *

LT 1 Semi-Open Area; occasional bushes

LT 97 Dense Vegetation (less than 50% of normal speed, forced to walk)

0.2 — Distinct Vegetation Boundary (along different wood types, fire breaks, cuts, small openings, etc.)

*If your printer has difficulty reproducing the LT 36 screen (10% density), use the next denser LT 37 (20%) instead.

# Selected
# Control Descriptions

This is only a partial assortment of the most frequently used control descriptions (codes). The best source for a complete listing we've found is in *Rastinmääritteet*, a booklet made available by the Finnish Orienteering Association—and conveniently published in four languages concurrently. The symbols as published show specific numbers for each—based on the various categories they appear under (1 plus for Terrain Forms, etc.). However, since these numbers are not standard, we have omitted them here.

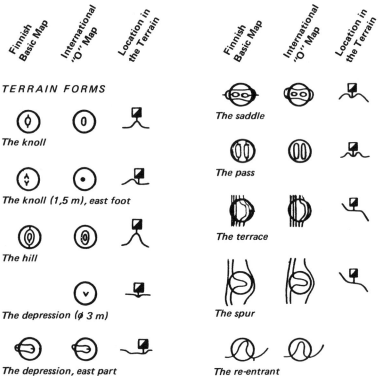

Finnish Basic Map   International "O" Map   Location in the Terrain       Finnish Basic Map   International "O" Map   Location in the Terrain

**TERRAIN FORMS**

*The knoll*

*The knoll (1,5 m), east foot*

*The hill*

*The depression (⌀ 3 m)*

*The depression, east part*

*The saddle*

*The pass*

*The terrace*

*The spur*

*The re-entrant*

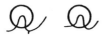

The re-entrant, upper end

The cliff foot

On the cliff, south end

### HYDROGRAPHIC FEATURES

The pond, west edge

The spring, west edge

The stream bend

The stream junction

The ditch end

### MARSHES

The marsh (ø 6 m)

The marsh, northwest part

The solid ground, northwest tip

### OPEN TERRAIN AND FORESTS

The field

The field, southeast corner

### SURFACE-ROCKS, STONES ETC.

The boulder (2 m), west side

The eastern boulder (2,8 m), east side

## COMMUNICATIONS

The path bend

The northern path bend

The path crossing

The path-stream crossing

## SETTLEMENTS AND BOUNDARIES

The building, east side

The ruin, west side

## ARTIFICIAL SHAPES

The pit (ø 3 m)

The gravel pit, east part

# Information
# Resources

Information about orienteering can be obtained in the form of brochures and *information sheets* from local and national organizations, *books* which can be purchased or borrowed from the library, and *films* which can be rented. The principal organization in the United States is the U. S. Orienteering Federation (P.O. Box #500, Athens, Ohio 45701); in Canada, it's the Canadian Orienteering Service (446 McNicoll Avenue, Willowdale, Ontario #M2H2E1).

The titles listed under *books* are only a partial list of those available —some dealing chiefly with the various aspects of map reading, compass use and/or competitive orienteering techniques; others with training ideas and procedures; still others with map making and other orienteering matters. Each carries a brief annotation to help direct the reader more nearly to the type of information he or she is seeking.

Under *films*, remember that local orienteering clubs can help in locating these; they often have films available for loan or rent.

## BOOKS

*Be Expert with Map & Compass* by Björn Kjellström (Charles Scribner's Sons, New York, NY; new edition, 1976). An excellent general handbook.

*Orienteering* by John Disley (Stackpole Books, Harrisburg, PA; 1973). A British title now popular in North America.

*Competitive Orienteering* by Hellman, Kaill, Rystedt and Gustavsson (Canadian Orienteering Service, Willowdale, Ontario; 1971). As the title suggests, intended for advanced "runners."

*Introduction to Orienteering* by Carlson, Lee, Peepre and Peepre (Canadian Orienteering Service, Willowdale, Ontario; 1972). Designed as a handbook for instructors.

*Teaching Orienteering* by James Gilchrist. (Canadian Orienteering Service; 1975). Another helpful instructor's manual.

*Orienteering Techniques* by Bertil Norman (British Orienteering Federation, Lea Green, Matlock, Derbyshire; 1975). More useful guidance on orienteering basics.

*Course Planning* by Sue Harvey (British Orienteering Federation; 1973). An English translation of a well known Swedish title on this important aspect of orienteering.

*Orienteering* by the Boy Scouts of America (BSA, New Brunswick, NJ; 1974). Aimed particularly at the younger orienteer.

*The Spur Book of Map & Compass* by Terry Brown and Rob Hunter (Spur Books, Ltd., Bourne End, Buckinghamshire, England; 1975). A truly pocket-size British title.

*Ski Orienteering* by Björn Kjellström (American Orienteering Service, Colorado Springs, CO [now the Orienteering Service/USA, LaPorte, IN]; 1974). A helpful and inexpensive booklet on this specialty.

*Mapmaking for Orienteers* by the British Orienteering Federation (B.O.F.; 1973). Good supplementary material on map making.

*Drawing Specifications for International Orienteering Maps* by the International Orienteering Federation (I.O.F., Upplands Vasby, Sweden; 1975). More basics for orienteering map makers.

*White Mountain Guide* by the Appalachian Mountain Club (AMC, Boston, MA; 1976). Contains new declination grids for orienteering.

*The New Aerobics* by Kenneth Cooper (Bantam Books, New York, NY; 1970). A good review of these excellent training exercises.

*Caldwell on Cross-Country* by John Caldwell (The Stephen Greene Press, Brattleboro, VT; 1975). The excellent material on training here applies equally well to competitive orienteering.

*Jogging: A Complete Physical Fitness Program for All Ages* by W. E. Harris (Grosset & Dunlap, New York, NY; 1973). Another good training manual.

*The New Cross-Country Ski Book* by John Caldwell (The Stephen Greene Press, Brattleboro, VT; 4th edition, 1973. Also available in a mass-paperback edition from Bantam Books and in a French-language edition from Les Éditions de L'Homme Ltée., Montreal, P.Q.) See especially the training chapter.

*The Snowshoe Book* by William Osgood and Leslie Hurley (The Stephen Greene Press, Brattleboro, VT; 2nd edition, 1975. Also available in a French-language edition from Les Éditions de L'Homme Ltée.) Solid information on winter cross-country travel.

## FILMS

*In the U.S.A.*

Orienteering Service/USA
P.O. Box 547
La Porte, IN    46350

Silva, Inc.
2466 State Road 39 N.
North LaPorte, IN    46350

International Film Bureau, Inc.
332 South Michigan Avenue
Chicago, IL    60604

*In Canada*

Canadian Orienteering Service
446 McNicoll Avenue
Willowdale, Ontario M2H 2 E1

Educational Film Distributors, Ltd.
285 Lesmill Road
Don Mills, Ontario M3B 2 V1

# Equipment
# Resources

Getting the various materials with which to prepare the maps for and/or run an orienteering meet should be no problem. A partial list of these sources follows. No doubt there are many others. Some local communities have considerable resource material for outdoor recreation available right at hand; service organizations such as the Boy and Girl Scouts are another good source. This list will likely expand considerably in future editions of *Orienteering for Sport and Pleasure* to include other helpful ideas not spelled out in this first edition.

## TOPOGRAPHIC MAPS

IN THE U.S.

The best procedure by which to obtain topographic maps from the U.S. Geological Survey—and it's a fairly new one at this writing—is a two-step one:

1. Request an index of topographic maps for the state in question from:
   > Branch of Distribution
   > U.S. Geological Survey
   > 1200 South Eads Street
   > Arlington, VA   22202
2. On receipt of the index, locate the particular quadrangle of interest and request this from:
   a. for maps *west* of the Mississippi River:
      > Branch of Distribution
      > U.S. Geological Survey
      > Federal Center
      > Denver, CO   80225
   b. for maps *east* of the Mississippi River:
      > Branch of Distribution
      > U.S. Geological Survey
      > 1200 Eads Street
      > Arlington, VA   22202

IN CANADA

For topographic maps information write:
> Map Distribution Office
> 615 Booth Street
> Ottawa, Ontario, K2E 6 N4

## OTHER MAP AND CHART INFORMATION

### IN THE U.S.

National Cartographic
  Information Center
507 National Center
Reston, VA   22092

### IN CANADA

Map Distribution Office
615 Booth Street
Ottawa, Ontario K2E 6 N4

## AERIAL PHOTOS

### IN THE U.S.

National Cartographic
  Information Center
507 National Center
Reston, VA   22092

One commercial source is:
  Aero Service Corporation
  4219 Van Kirk Street
  Philadelphia, PA   19135

### IN CANADA

National Air Photo Library
615 Booth Street (Room 110)
Ottawa, Ontario K2E 6 N4

## SOURCES FOR MAKING O-BASE MAPS

Karttjänst
Box 83
S-66001 ED
Sweden

Bakken & Helgesen
Boks 50
N-3425 Reistad
Norway

## MEET SUPPLIES

### IN THE U.S.

Orienteering Service/USA
P.O. Box 547
La Porte, IN   46350

Nordic Traders
Little Pond Road
Londonderry, VT   05148

Silva, Inc.
2466 State Road 39 N.
North LaPorte, IN   46350

Recreational Equipment, Inc.
P.O. Box 22088
Seattle, WA   98122

Eastern Mountain Sports, Inc.
1041 Commonwealth Avenue
Boston, MA   02215

The Ski Hut
P.O. Box 309
Berkeley, CA   94701

Eddie Bauer
P.O. Box 3700
Third & Virginia
Seattle, WA   98124

### IN CANADA

Canadian Orienteering Services
446 McNicoll Avenue
Willowdale, Ontario M2H 2 E1

# Index

"O-" or "O" has been used for the word *orienteering* almost exclusively throughout the Index.